Women of the HARVEST

Inspiring Stories of Contemporary Farmers

Profiles by Holly L. Bollinger, Susan Gartner,
Lauren Heaton, and Bethany Weaver-Culpepper
Foreword by MaryJane Butters

Photography by Cathy Phillips

Dedication
To the women farmers of the past, present, and future.

FRONTIS:
Rose Koenig tends to the flowers in her Gainesville, Florida, garden.

TITLE PAGE:
Peggy Case rakes hay on her ranch outside of Pagosa Springs, Colorado.

ON THE COVER:
Michelle Bienick and her husband Brian operate a seven-acre farm in the Applegate River Valley in Oregon.

BACK COVER:
(top left) Sarah Polyock prepares a bottle for one of her calves on her dairy farm near Chetek, Wisconsin.

(top right) For the past 20 years, Jana Sweets has owned and operated Sticky Situation desert plant farm and nursery.

(bottom) Lini Mazumdar and her husband, Emmett, are the proprietors of Anjali Farms, a certified organic farm in South Londonderry, Vermont, which also includes Lotus Moon Medicinals.

First published in 2007 by Voyageur Press, an imprint of MBI Publishing Company LLC, Galtier Plaza, Suite 200, 380 Jackson Street, St. Paul, MN 55101-4810 USA

Copyright © 2007 by Holly L. Bollinger and Catherine Lee Phillips

Voyageur Press titles are also available at discounts in bulk quantity for industrial or sales-promotional use. For details write to Special Sales Manager at MBI Publishing Company, Galtier Plaza, Suite 200, 380 Jackson Street, St. Paul, MN 55101-4810 USA.

To find out more about our books, join us online at www.voyageurpress.com.

Library of Congress Cataloging-in-Publication Data

Bollinger, Holly, 1972-
  Women of the harvest : inspiring stories of contemporary farmers / by Holly L. Bollinger and Cathy Phillips.
    p. cm.
  Includes index.
  ISBN-13: 978-0-7603-2184-3 (hc w/ jacket)
  ISBN-10: 0-7603-2184-1 (hc w/ jacket)
  1. Women farmers--United States. 2. Women in agriculture--United States. I. Phillips, Catherine Lee, 1958- II. Title.
  HD6077.2.U6B65 2007
  630.92'273--dc22
                                    2006028781

Editor: Amy Glaser
Designer: Sara Holle

Printed in China

CONTENTS

Foreword
By MaryJane Butters

If I could have read this book 20 years ago when I first announced I wanted to be a farmer by laying claim to five acres of my own at the end of a dirt road in Idaho, I wouldn't have felt so utterly alone at times—alone when I couldn't manage my bills, alone when a banker asked if there were any men in my life who would be willing to co-sign the agricultural operating loan I had applied for, alone after chopping thistle for days in the pouring rain or searing sun, alone when an unprecedented flood washed out my crops and mile-long road.

Today, women are the fastest growing group of people buying and operating small farms. While the number of American farms has dropped 14 percent in the last 25 years, the number of farms run by women has increased 86 percent! At this rate, some predict that within another 10 years, women may own as much as 75 percent of the farmland in the United States.

Like a tenacious new breed of invasive weed, we're here to stay; laying down roots and growing right where we've always belonged. The 17 women profiled in this ground-breaking book are typical of this "new breed," this "different" kind of farmer the media is talking about. Our approach to agriculture is more holistic and systematic. Instead of buying what we can spray from a nozzle to fix a problem today, we take the long view. The homemade farm sign at the beginning of my lane says: "Living like we'll die tomorrow, farming like we'll live forever."

From the women in this book, you'll learn that women farmers aren't interested in commodity agriculture and the latest new chemical or genetically engineered wonder.

We're not dreaming of endless frontiers. Instead, we're giving new meaning to the term "value-added." We're expanding the boundaries of food distribution and the definition of farm. We're pushing the limits of marketing. We're busy feeding our neighbors and friends and families through Community Supported Agriculture programs and at farmers' markets.

With incredible ingenuity, we're feeding our creative urges. When we raise lambs for sale, we give lessons on spinning and knitting. When we grow the ingredients for salsa, we hold Latin dance clinics. When we promote the sale of our crops as ingredients perfect for pizza, we plant our vegetables in wedges that form a grand circle when seen from afar. When we grow 60 different sunflower bouquets, we take photos for a line of sunny greeting cards. When we decide to convert land into native prairie again, we turn it into a business that sells and promotes endangered native plants. When we open up our hearts, we open up our homes and turn them into bed-and-breakfast sanctuaries where our guests are fed the best food on earth.

We're all over the Internet, blogging and advertising our food. We make handmade goods, such as wooden clothes racks and button jewelry to supplement our farm incomes. We're active participants in problem-solving Internet chatrooms. We're notorious seed savers. We love to grow heirloom varieties of plants. We milk 6 to 60 cows, not 6,000, and we're known for our artisan cheeses. We're the spirit of the beehive and we love ventures that allow us to cross-pollinate ideas with other women farmers.

We're a force—a force of nature. We're drawn to farming because of the sensory, tactile nature of it. We want to feel our lives and taste them and truly live them. I predict that in the same manner historians refer to life before and after the industrial revolution, we'll go down in history as key players in the new millennium's farming revolution—to be known as the era at the turn of the century when women collectively changed the face of agriculture.

If you're a land-poor female farmer longing for your place in the country, take heart. The types of ground breaking women featured in this book are creating a growing demand for local, hands-on food. Or like 95-year-old Eloise Stewart, the matriarch of a tree farm located in Florida, raising the business bar by creating one of the best-managed, environmentally sensitive tree farms in America. I call them "intimate crops," or one-on-one food.

Twenty years ago, not enough people in my locale cared that my bell peppers, pickling cucumbers, canning tomatoes, and garlic were organically grown and nurtured from start to finish with love and care. What mattered most was the price. What matters now is the name—it's MaryJane's garlic.

Fifteen years ago, I didn't have the support of politicians like I did five years ago when I was voted Idaho's Progressive Business Person of the Year. In fact, when I applied for status as Idaho's first organic food manufacturer in the early 1990s, I was turned down. "We don't want you putting the word 'organic' on your food," said a politician with strong ties to big business. "When you use the word 'organic', you charge more for it, making it seem like your food is better than ours."

Agriculture is changing—a change that has a female voice, not just from female farmers, but from mothers concerned about safe food and women who've come to realize how much better they feel when they eat better. But the backbone of a kinder, gentler agriculture has been strengthened by people like the pioneers in this book—women who can't resist the nurture part of their nature. Admittedly, some of the changes have been hard-won, but after 20 years, I can fervently claim the rewards pile up faster than manure!

Women who give in to their farm fantasies (I've never met a woman yet who hasn't, at some point in her life, had a farm fantasy) are in for a sensory journey like none other. Digging in the soil makes you whole. It's as simple and as complicated as that.

As our numbers grow, so does the abundance of opportunities and ideas. Sit back, read, and be inspired. There's a whole new frontier awaiting us, but it starts here, armed with the inspiration of women farmers who've already landed their dream.

Introduction

Maud Powell relaxes among her plants in her greenhouse outside of Jacksonville, Oregon.

Farming in the United States was once a prosperous occupation that fed the nation. Yet, it has undergone a change in the past 20 years. The family farms that date back to the 1800s were spread across the country, but now many have been bought by large-scale farms or sold for the land to become strip malls and subdivisions.

Despite the decline, there are stoic farmers who won't give up, no matter the odds, and are keeping the family farm alive. Many have left their cubicles in the city to move to the country, grow their own vegetables, raise animals, get back to the basics, and be more in tune with nature. Of these farmers, the number of women either working or operating the farm is steadily increasing. According to the 2002 U.S. Census of Agriculture, 27 percent of the just over 3 million farmers are women. Women are the primary operators of about 11 percent of the farms, which is a 13.4 percent increase from the 1997 data.

The women profiled in this book work on farms with specialties ranging from dairy farming to maintaining a vineyard and bottling wine to growing and processing chiles. These 17 women love farming as well as the connection it provides between the land and animals to their souls. Michelle feels the pulse of the earth as she sinks her hands into the dirt and weeds around her vegetables. Laura feels most in tune with the world when she is knee-deep in the Gulf of Mexico planting clam seeds. At sunset, Nancy is astride her horse on the highest point of her ranch in the Cascade Mountains while she drinks in the scents of sage and juniper berries around her and counts her blessings. Each of them has her hardships and bad days. Yet, in the end, it's the perseverance and dedication that makes these women stand up, wipe the sweat off their brows, and invest every available ounce of energy into their farms.

Patricia Orlowitz

Washington, D.C.

By Holly L. Bollinger

Patricia Orlowitz stands beside a sign next to a newly dedicated road in Rubovc, Kosovo. The road was built thanks to the help of the U.S. Agency for International Development. Jack Evans

When someone you love leaves home on an U.S. aid mission to handle a little paperwork for family farmers in a mountainous European country, you don't worry that she's going to stay. You just say, "See you!" and hope that you see her sooner rather than later.

At least that's what everyone who loves Patricia Orlowitz thought. At the age of 38, she packed a few suitcases, kissed and hugged her family and friends, and said good-bye to her whole world to help others in a world she'd never known anything about.

"Moldova?" she asked herself. "Where is that?"

She left as Patty, a professional businesswoman and seasoned communicator with decades of writing, marketing, and public relations experience in the American agricultural industry. What she discovered on her brief stay in January 1997 changed her life, as well as the lives of her loved ones and those of more than a million Moldovans, forever.

Patty was raised by her parents in the Detroit suburb of Birmingham, Michigan. Her father, Bob Wilde, was an editor of an engineering magazine. Originally from Chicago, her mom, Mary, was a frequently published writer for several magazines and newspapers.

Patty and her older sister Cathy spent many holidays and summer vacations at their grandparents' farm near Waterloo, Iowa. Early on, they learned about the toil Grandpa Wilde endured on his farm. Patty grew up knowing that family farmers worked a huge amount of their own sweat and blood into the fields that they farmed season after season.

10

The sign reads:

USAID
FROM THE AMERICAN PEOPLE

Mercy Corps

Municipal Infrastructure and Support Initiative

This **Road Asphalting Project** is made possible through the generosity of the American people, the local community and the municipality.

Stefan Zderea, one of Moldova's proud private farmers, grows potatoes, corn, wheat, sunflower, watermelons, and other crops on his land. Jack Evans

Her grandfather was a tenant farmer in early 1900s. He worked landowners' farms for many years before he was able to buy his own farm in the 1930s. Seeing her grandfather work his 260 acres gave Patty a sense of pride about farming that only first-hand experience could give a young, modern woman from a professional suburbanite family. That pride led her into a career of agricultural communications, launched by a degree to match from Michigan State University.

Patty was nearly incredulous when she at first heard about the plight of Moldovan farmers. It's a predominantly Slavic country, just slightly larger than the state of Massachusetts, nestled in the rolling hills between Romania and the Ukraine. Small farming communities make up the majority of its population, which is near 4.5

Patricia stands alongside Stefan Zderea, who is a farmer in the village of Saiti, Moldova. He's now a private farmer thanks to the privatization program.
Jack Evans

million. For generations stretching back into the 1600s, the Moldovan people have devoted their lives to agriculture.

In more recent times, those families were systematically stripped of their heritage as subsistence farmers and were oppressed by their own government. During the early 1960s, the political entity that was the Soviet Union took away their land and reduced them to mere tenant workers on lands they had inherited centuries ago.

When Patty first arrived in the country in 1997, it had been almost 50 years since Communism's collective farm structure quickly swept away the Moldovans' civil rights. Although they were barred from owning the land they worked, the farmers of Moldova—and their ancestors—had worked too hard for too many years not to love those lands and stay on them.

A singer (left) from a village Orthodox church choir in northern Moldova, competing in a festival in the Soroca fortress, offers vin de casa *(homemade wine) to Fortress curator and historian Nicolae Bulat (center) and visitors Lois Evans and Patricia Orlowitz. There's not an occasion in Moldova that passes without a toast, as Moldovans like to express their thoughts and welcome people to their homes. Jack Evans*

Then, with the fall of Communism in 1991, Moldovans regained their independence, but what could they do with it? The government still owned their land. How were they supposed to get it back? Men and women farmers alike had their freedom, but they had no money or legal assistance to help them buy back their rightful inheritances. Time and society—even a newly liberated one—had forgotten the people inside Moldovan agriculture. Most Moldovan farmers did not own enough of anything to be considered as collateral, nor did they have the cash flow to obtain loans from any traditional type of bank.

"It would probably have struck my grandfather that farm life in Moldova is awfully close to what his life was like on the farm in the early 1900s," Patty told *People* magazine in 2000, when she was featured in an Up Front story about her adventure.

Patty's initial short trip from the United States had been to help with a U.S. Agency for International Development (USAID) accounting project, and it ended after a few months. Later that year, she was headed into another USAID opportunity that spanned into the next century.

Patty joined an organization called the Center for Private Business Reform (CPBR). Her mostly Moldovan CPBR teammates, more than 250 of them; her two American colleagues; and Patty worked tirelessly to find a solution for farmers without

money. They searched to find ways for the Moldovan farmers to use their new democratic resources and buy the lands they continued to farm for the government.

The idea of setting up savings and credit associations came up several years earlier through the CPBR and other international assistance agencies about the time of Moldova's independence from Soviet rule. However, the first 11 associations were not established until 1997, and the CPBR was one of them.

The Moldovan agricultural assistance project was initiated through a nationwide effort called the Alliance for Rural Microfinancing of Moldova. In 2000, the CPBR gave the Alliance a grant to help implement the project. In her official capacity as CPBR deputy general director, Patty told the media, "The Moldova Microfinancing Alliance makes an excellent team. They have proven their skills, and therefore, we support them."

In her heart, though, Patty was dealing with much more powerful emotions for the families who were fulfilling lifelong dreams of harvesting their own lands. "Owning land is necessary for a democratic society," she says. "When I came here I thought, 'This is something I believe in passionately.'"

By then, Patty already had learned a lot about life in Moldova. She had to overcome a language barrier between English and the native Romanian tongue, so she

Across Kosovo, in addition to houses in all stages of construction, are covered soccer playing fields, including this new one being erected in southeastern Kosovo near Macedonia. Ruins of homes damaged in the 1998-1999 armed conflict remain as depressing reminders of the tension between ethnic groups, but new homes are rising throughout the area. Patricia Orlowitz

The caretaker of the tomb of Sultan Murat I, Ottoman emperor who was killed in the 1389 Battle of Kosovo, offered Patricia Orlowitz a tour of the tomb, which has been watched by her family's descendants for generations. Learning more about local history and culture is one of the advantages of living abroad. Patricia Orlowitz

learned to speak Romanian. Next, Patty had to gain a better understanding of the personal histories behind the millions of lives that had been invested working in the unforgiving Moldovan climate. Families often returned from the fields to cold, dark houses without heat and power. "There was a lack of heat in most public buildings, so I'd go to meetings wearing my boots, my tights, and my long underwear," Patty says. Even today, the wealthiest of rural families may only have electricity for a few hours each week.

To find a place inside the warm hearts of Moldovan communities, she had to become one of them, which wasn't an easy task. In Soviet days, Moldovan children were raised to believe that all Americans had horrific faces to match their evil nature.

Americans were monsters, not people. Those children, now grown, were the same people Patty had to befriend in order to empower them.

Her nicknames—Patty or Pat—didn't resonate as respectable titles for a woman in Moldova; they were too American-sounding so she returned to her birth name, Patricia. Then she began to learn and live many of the Old World customs that defined the Moldovan culture. Finally, Patricia had to learn the law and how to legally help this freed society. They needed to gain power over their own lands so they could decide for themselves how to invest in producing the crops, livestock, and agricultural products that served their families best.

It was a good start to her group's project that the now-democratic government (albeit the first of the formerly Soviet democracies to elect a Communist president in 2001, re-electing him in 2005) was already seeking ways to help with the privatization of the country's farms. Eventually, the collaborative efforts of governments and citizens began paying off. Patricia's work brought a new sense of pride in farming to her and the millions of lives she touched in Moldova.

From 1998 to 2001, the CPBR, mostly through the work of Patricia's team and the resilient Moldovan people, successfully privatized more than 1,000 collective

On July 4, 2000, Stefan Zderea received title to his land in Saiti, a village in southwestern Moldova, near Ukraine. Stefan, in his 70s, remembers being a teenager when his mother (his father was killed in World War II) gave the land to the collective farm rather than face deportation. Sixteen families were forcibly deported in July 1949, and the next day his mother told him, "We have no choice; we want to stay together, here, as a family, so I'm going to the kolkhoz to give it our land and our cows." Jack Evans

A natural spring in the mountains of Kosovo, near Montenegro, is channeled into a handmade trough, catching it for easier use. People will come to the springs and fill up bottles or buckets with the water. The shepherds bring sheep and cows to this area for four months of summer grazing. Kosovo's wood craftsmanship is good, though illegal logging is reducing the forests, as people cut trees for firewood. Patricia Orlowitz

farms. Post-privatization efforts continue through programs that educate farmers and local authorities in rural areas of the country. The effects of Patricia's well-done pioneering job continue to be as potent to the Moldovan farmers today as they were ten years ago.

As Patricia explains it, whenever a titling ceremony is held, it's as though the countrymen and women of Moldova are being given a coveted award of some kind. From the first land title granted to the millionth, Moldovan farmers are both elated and awed to own their livelihood.

"People walk forward to receive their titles and you see the tears in their eyes," she reminisces. "It's kept in a place of honor. I've seen farmers keep it behind the homes' religious icon. It is treasured."

Growing a Moldovan Money Tree

Building a money-lending association in Moldova is a painstaking process done under the country's strict laws on Savings and Credit Associations of Citizens. A minimum number of 10 members is needed up front. The first step is for the proposed association's members to organize a constitutional meeting.

During the meeting, the future members must officially decide upon the creation of the association and adopt its formal charter. Then they have to submit the documents to the Ministry of Justice to obtain the necessary state registration. All of that allows the association to get its money-handling license from the state supervision service.

Members of a savings and credit association can live in or move to the same village or town that agrees upon the association's "principles of financial intra-assistance and of members' mutual responsibility." Once it is founded, charter members make cash deposits that give the association its operating capital.

The members have equal responsibilities and possibilities. Each of them has one vote, regardless of the amount of money they deposit into the association's capital. Similar associations exist in more than 100 countries worldwide. They are known under different names, such as credit associations, credit unions, and mutual support houses.

The original alliance that Patricia's organization, the CPBR, helped finance continues to offer training and assistance to the members of savings and credit associations with obtaining loans. It strives to maintain good relations with other organizations and banks that contribute to the implementation of the microfinancing project in Moldova.

Today there are close to 400 associations helping the Moldovan farm families, whose labors account for 60 percent of the nation's economy.

Lini Mazumdar

South Londonderry, Vermont

By Holly L. Bollinger

Lini Mazumdar and her husband, Emmett, are the proprietors of Anjali Farms, a certified organic farm in South Londonderry, Vermont, which also includes Lotus Moon Medicinals.

OPPOSITE PAGE:
Balance in all aspects of one's life is important to Lini. She occasionally teaches classes on healthy living, herbal remedies, and Indian cooking.

While the namesakes suggest peace and wisdom of the far-Eastern cultures from which they were adapted, Anjali Farms and Lotus Moon Medicinals are only as far east as the Green Mountains of Vermont.

Nestled on nine acres of a lush hillside just above the White River in South Londonderry, village herbalist Lini Mazumdar grows and prepares medicinal plants. Along with her husband, Emmett, she also produces certified organic fruits and vegetables—all of which she says make up a portion of the equation for healing her customers inside and out.

"People have to realize that they do get sick from what they put into their bodies," says Lini. "If you get sick, you can't just take an herbal pill to get better. You have to really go back and look at everything—your lifestyle, what you're putting into your body food-wise, medicine-wise, everything-wise, your relationships, everything. It's just a balance of a whole because you are a whole person."

According to Lini, medicinal plants can basically be described as "Things that you don't necessarily use for food or for common sale, unless you're using them for medicinal purposes." Like many of the uncultivated varieties native to the state, some just grow on their own. "A lot of them grow here as weeds—dandelions, valerian, echinacea," she says. "I've introduced a bunch of new species that aren't from here, but that will grow in our zone."

Lini and Emmett sell their vegetables and flowers at various farmers' markets in the area.

Lini met her husband Emmett in 1997 while he was managing a California farmers' market and she was working for a Tibetan doctor. She says that as they began sharing their ideas and dreams (he wanted to farm and she wanted to study herbs), they quickly realized how much they had in common.

Within just a couple weeks of meeting, both of their jobs coincidentally ended and Lini was free to pursue her interests in herbs. "I started studying herbs with different herbalists and then finally one of them said, 'You know, if you're really serious about this as you seem to be, why don't you go to school for (herbal studies)?' And so I did," she says.

Lini studied at the Southwestern School of Botanical Medicine in Bisbee, Arizona, to add to her undergraduate and graduate degrees in counseling psychology. "I started learning a lot (about herbs) before that, but that's where I culminated my studies in (the medicinal) area." She went through the residency program in 1998 and spent five months in an intensive hands-on curriculum. Soon after her residency ended, she became a certified herbalist.

In the meantime, Emmett had met another California farmers' market manager who had started an organic farm in Vermont and needed someone to manage it while he was away. Emmett took the chance to learn more about hands-on farming practices and moved to Vermont.

Lini and Emmett kept in touch through the mail. One day he wrote to Lini and asked her to come back east and grow herbs on the Wild Farm in Arlington, Vermont. She accepted his offer and the two have been together ever since. "A very, very random series of events," Lini reminisces. "But both of our dreams were realized within one another. It took a little bit of time to happen, but they happened."

The couple stayed on the farm for three years before they decided it was time to find their own place. Lini says they knew they had to put their energies into their own property because organic farming was such a big investment with very delayed returns. They searched for a farm for quite awhile, but they couldn't find a place that was both affordable and suitable. Many farm possibilities had been previously laden with pesticide chemicals that contaminated the soils for their organic approach.

Emmett bought a greenhouse because he knew he would use it on their farm someday. Lini says something occurred to Emmett as he dismantled the greenhouse and began moving the pieces to his mother's property in South Londonderry for storage in her barn. He kept looking over the peaceful and familiar land, and he was thinking maybe that was the place for their farm.

"We'd never even thought about this area because it was much higher in elevation and much farther north than we were looking. But this is a property that his mother and father bought 28 years ago and it's been in the family ever since," says Lini. Because Emmett grew up there, he knew the land had been fallow for decades and that it would be safe for an organic farm. Lini laughs when she thinks back to her first impression about the location, "I said, 'Gosh it's so cold up here.'"

Although the farm is only a short distance from where they had originally considered establishing a farm, Lini says they immediately lost a whole month of their growing season because of the altitude. Anjali Farms is in almost an entirely different growing zone from Arlington, which means it faces two extra weeks of frost before the spring season takes hold and the cold of autumn settles in two weeks earlier as well. Mostly, says Lini, the temperature change posed a challenge for the organic heirloom vegetables they grow. "Herbs are really, really strong," she adds. "They're perennial and they can grow all over in most types of soil. But we adapted; we learned; we have greenhouses."

The couple farms three of their nine acres, including about one-quarter of an acre that Lini uses for her medicinal business. She rotates her herbs to different parts of the farm from year to year and says that many of the medicinal plants she grows readily adapt—even to rocky soils. Weeds are usually her biggest problem, and those typically come from straggling hay seeds.

Lini and Emmett also raise about 80 free-range and laying chickens, which they allow to roam on a portion of the fallow land until it's substantially worn and fertilized. Then they move the flock to another area for a while. Lini says she has more of an attachment to her chickens than most farmers probably do. "I don't really like having livestock on the farm; it's too personal. But the eggs are really important because it allows our whole farm to have life in a sense," she says optimistically. Per the certified organic standards, Lini says most of the chicken manure is composted for a year and then used as fertilizer for the growing areas.

During the late summer months, Lini prepares her medicinal products for the rest of the year and makes tinctures, oils, and salves or hanging plants in her drying room. Lini's herbal healing products sell all through the winter, but Christmas is her busiest season. She also attends craft shows and local events throughout the year, but avoids going too far during the winter. "The last time I went [to Boston], we had an amazingly huge snow storm that I had to drive back in," she recounts. "It took me six hours to get home and I said, 'I don't think I'll do this show anymore.'"

Lini and Emmett take their produce to the local farmers' market and routinely sell their products in the local health food store, as well as to organic-friendly restaurants throughout the area. Lini occasionally teaches classes, either co-teaching with other people or hosting a series of classes on the farm about the value of healthy eating and herbal remedies. "I also teach Indian cooking because I feel like it's not just herbs that contribute to our health, but it's food that contributes to our

Lini grows herbs to make her own salves and tinctures for Lotus Moon Medicinals.

Lini and Emmett sell foods that are in season at their farm and at farmers' markets, as well as to the local health food store and local organic-friendly restaurants. They want to emphasize that people need to pay attention to the seasons and eat what is currently in season to experience the true taste of the food.

health," she stresses. "Food is medicine. I've been incorporating some of that into my teachings as well."

Lini and Emmett practice, but aren't yet certified, in biodynamic farming. "Biodynamic is one step deeper than organics where people practice with the moon cycles. You will grow or harvest your plants according to the moon cycles. It's really fascinating," she says. "We're definitely going to get certified in biodynamics eventually, but right now we definitely practice many things. We go by the calendar."

She explains that for every day of the year, the biodynamic calendar indicates whether it's a good day to work the land, and if so, what types of work should be done with which areas. On an unfavorable day, she does office work or something else around the farm. Although the calendar's advice doesn't always fit her seasonal issues, Lini says sometimes it is very specific. "It says, 'Today's a good day for fruit,' so I work with berries. It's a good day to work with the berries or pick the berries." Other biodynamic techniques include treating the water used to irrigate the produce using ingredients from some of her on-farm plants to increase the nutritional benefits, such as raising nitrogen levels.

Lini says that although most serious organic growers are aware of biodynamics, not all organic farmers are prepared to push themselves to meet the time-intensive measures of biodynamic standards. She believes it's the same situation in straight organic farming.

"A lot of people say, 'I grow things organically,' but this doesn't mean they're certified organic. A certified organic farm is really different. [Every year] Emmett and I, right around tax time, have to sit down and finish a 25-page application that certifies our farm. It's the worst time to do it and it's a lot of money and our time and energy. But we still have to do it for the success of the [certified organic] movement."

Lini says the certification paperwork, due annually on April 15, is packed full of in-depth questions. "What we've grown, how we've grown them, where we've grown them, how we've rotated, what we sprayed on them, what we haven't sprayed on them, what we picked, when we picked—it's so, so detailed," says Lini. "It's very maddening that organic farmers have to prove themselves clean, whereas conventional farmers can do anything and get pesticides to spray any [chemical] on [the crops]."

Lini attributes part of the abundance of chemical pesticides used on U.S. farms to the American way of life and our overall value system. "This culture feels that food should be cheap and not cost much of anything. Other countries are not like that— food has a value to it," she says.

"Especially coming from India, where we eat seasonal foods because we don't have the huge refrigeration systems and transportation systems across the country. We don't transport northern fruits to the south or winter foods during the summer season. But here, you can get strawberries from South America in the wintertime, even tomatoes in the wintertime. It's so absurd. And our bodies don't even crave that. Eating foods seasonally is so much healthier for you, and eating foods locally grown is so much healthier for you. And then, of course, eating food organically is so much healthier for you." But not at the cost of shipping them across the country, Lini adds.

"People don't practice the seasons anymore. They don't listen to their bodies in the different seasons when various foods of the season are important to your health." Lini believes today's society has lost a great deal of appreciation for the fresh produce of each season. "Everything is diluted when you can get strawberries and blueberries and raspberries in the winter. Then, they're not as good, but people forget what good is and what true taste is."

Lini points out that some people's bodies are warm-natured and need heavier, warmer foods, and some people require cooler foods to eat. "A lot of people want to just eat salad all the time, and it's not right for some people's bodies."

The chickens on Lini's farm roam in a certain area until the land is properly fertilized and cultivated. Then they are moved to a different area of the farm for the same purpose.

Lini and Emmett live on a farm that Emmett's parents bought 28 years ago. Even though it's farther north than the original location they were considering, they have adapted and use greenhouses to help their growing season.

Lini, and other nutritional herbalists like her, work to teach people the differences in their own bodies and the importance of differences in the types of foods they eat. "That's a lot of our quest, is to really make people realize that it is one year and there are seasons. There are times when we do this and then when we should not do this," she says.

It's realistic to say that Lini's ideals are rooted in her Eastern Indian culture. She says that although there are plenty of herbalists in the United States, not all of them subscribe to the idea of treating a whole person—not just through remedies—and starting with nutrition.

"There are lots of herbalists in Vermont doing the Western herbal thing. And I think they're doing various aspects of it. A bunch of them are midwives, some of them are just practicing herbalists, and some of them are just growing." She adds that her approach is fairly unique in the area. "I think the whole nutritional thing is pretty new. I think herbalists are still trying to take care of [health] problems by giving herbs, right? I'm trying to go back one step further, one step beyond, so that you don't have to do herbs, you can do things with your food and be preventative with your food— or, if you are ill already, so that you don't have to take herbs; you might just watch what you're eating. It's not [just] that I think this, it's a fact that your food is medicine."

Three acres of the farm are used for growing vegetables, plants, flowers, and herbs.

Donna Betts

Whipple, Ohio

By Holly L. Bollinger

Donna Betts has farmed her 200-acre farm for the past 40 years without the use of any chemicals. Donna is a strong believer in sustainable farming methods and she serves as a mentor for other farmers.

OPPOSITE PAGE:
Donna is strong-willed and doesn't let anything get in her way. In 1965, she was the first woman in Ohio to qualify for the federal Farmers Home Administration loan. She bought the farm where she still lives and works.

When you reach the answering machine for Ohio Appalachian farmer Donna Betts, a wise and pleasant voice greets you with: "Hello, this is Donna Betts at Gwamma's Farm where we take you back to the future of farming—while factory farms are out and real food family farms are in. You know the drill for a message. And remember, you are what you eat."

Donna's way is to always speak her mind, and when it comes to her 50-plus years of first-hand farming know-how, Donna's approach to conversation becomes infused with just the right touch of what-for. She wastes no time imparting to people she meets that what's good for each of us is good for all of us—and no more so than when it comes to living with the food we grow and eat.

While Donna's farming ideas may seem like old-fashioned ideals to some modern consumers, they reflect the traditional healthy practices that millions of American families have lived by for many generations. Donna believes that sustainable farming methods such as hers have ensured the longevity of our society to date. One glimpse at the verve in Donna's eyes tells you she's got something right.

"What you see is what you get," she says, commenting on her own unique style of dress. "Everything I wear is how people see me." Donna has worn many hats in the tight-knit farming community of north central Appalachia and throughout her life, from a young bride and mother to a farmer and activist. "I've known many people, and

Donna helped form Marietta Kitchen Creations (MKC) so that local growers can prepare and preserve their own produce by commercially acceptable standards. Then they can sell their locally produced products to the consumers in their communities.

people know me as many different things." There's rarely middle ground when it comes to Donna's reputation. She says that usually "They're either very much in favor of what I do, or they think I'm the plague."

For nearly 40 years, Donna has worked the couple hundred acres of land where she now lives without using chemicals as fertilizers or pesticides. She raised eight children there, often with the littlest in tow during her daily chores and nonstop farm duties. As her family flourished into adulthood, so did her farm and her views on farming.

"Years ago, whenever anyone had a question about gardening or raising livestock, they would go ask their grandparents who still lived on the farm," reads the opening paragraph of her self-produced Gwamma's Farm Retreat brochure. "Today, many people are seeking such expertise as they become interested in getting started in farming or just trying to become more self-sufficient and grow their own safe, healthy food.

"But few experts remain today that remember how things were done before the advent of modern agribusiness and chemical farming. People need more than informative books and how-to videos. They need specific, hands-on instruction and practical first-hand experience."

That's where Donna offers a helping hand. Today her Gwamma's Farm operation consists of a variety of crops and livestock raised in a way that makes up a truly diversified farming system on 80 of the 200 acres that she owns in Whipple, Ohio. She practices rotational grazing as part of a tricounty grazers' group. She raises and tends a 17-head herd of Belted Galloway cattle for breeding and beef, 20 ewes, dairy goats, and a couple of sows. Her organic vegetable garden benefits greatly from the manure that comes from her animals. She takes the milk from her goats and makes it into delicious cheeses. Every Saturday, Donna packs up most of her on-farm products to sell at the local farmers' market that she helped establish in the nearby town of Marietta in 1998.

It's in running the daily gamut of farming, harvesting, and marketing that Donna is willing to share her skills with interested farm and nonfarm families. It doesn't matter if newcomers are simply trying to gain a better perspective on sustainable agriculture or they want to build a chemical-free farming system, Donna is ready to tell and show them what it's all about.

She offers nearly year-round workshops and on-farm internships to those who participate in a Gwamma's Farm Retreat. She even has room and board available in the big red barn near the house. Participants come to Donna at all ages with all levels of farm experience. All are eager to learn from Donna, and she is just as eager to learn from them.

Recently a Michigan family of interns—father, mother, and their 10-year-old and infant daughters—stayed with Donna for two consecutive summers to learn more about how they can start their own sustainable family farm. Career changes were the initial catalyst for their gravitation to sustainable farming. Donna is now a regular household name in their family and she considers them a part of her ever-growing Gwamma's Farm family.

Donna wasn't born into a farm family. Quite the contrary, she's the product of a practical, yet industrious, family from Marietta. Her parents operated their own burial vault business. Donna remembers her father often enlisting the help of his children at the end of the week so he didn't have to pay the hired help overtime wages. "On the weekends, I went with Dad because I was the biggest and a tomboy," she says, adding that her dad frequently played ball with her in the front yard. He taught his athletic daughter how throw hardballs and fastballs, something most local girls couldn't have cared less about.

Her mother encouraged Donna's musical abilities. Donna began playing piano at the age of 5. By the fourth grade, she was an organist at a town church, and by the fifth grade, she had a paying job with another local congregation playing the day's popular, but cumbersome, pump organ.

In listening to Donna reminisce, even briefly, about her childhood, it's apparent she was always an independent and forward thinker. Voted the best athlete out of 204 students in her graduating class, Donna couldn't participate on a team because inter-scholastic sports weren't available.

Donna wanted to take vocational agricultural classes in high school, but the teacher refused to bring a girl into the class because of his sensitivity to teaching certain realities of farming, such as breeding livestock. It was appropriate retribution for Donna when her own teenage daughter became the first female to enter that same teacher's vo-ag classroom years later.

Every step of Donna's life has been taken with an even-keeled stride. Each new day reflects the experiences and knowledge that she's gained from many days before. She raised her eight children, from two of three marriages, as a farm wife. Donna says she learned early on that taking care of herself and her children meant being as self-sufficient in the business aspect as in the dirt-to-delivery production of farming.

In 1965, Donna became the first woman in Ohio to qualify for the federal Farmers Home Administration loan and she bought the 200-acre farm where she still lives and works. "This past winter, I decided, 'Okay, ten years ago I did my estate planning,' and I said then that 'I needed to take care of the rest of everything.' And it took me ten years to get around to it again. You could say I'm a procrastinator.

"So I've done a lot of work on [my family history] because I realized that my kids didn't know what I did when I was a young girl and growing up—and even when they were little. So I did do an outline of my autobiography." True to her form, Donna hedges a bit and finishes, "I think the expansion of that into something that's legible and would make sense will have to wait for this winter.

"But I've pulled out pictures and I wrote on the back of them. When my parents died 23 years ago, that was a lament that Mother hadn't done that. I was the oldest one and I recognized pictures that my two younger sisters didn't and I thought, 'Now, well that's foolish.' So I just got over the procrastination thing, and I figured that the next step was just to do it."

Donna poses with the Gravel Road Gang, a group of women that she mentors on Gwamma's Farm.

Donna doesn't mix sentimentality with the need for her own family's self-preservation. Her thoughts on dying—someday—are as fundamentally practical as her desire to live practically each day.

"This winter I had my son help set my coffin together," Donna says without even a hint of morbid pretense. "Only I've just gotten the last coat put on it—of polyurethane, and it's cherry from off our farm. My son just brought it outside of the door, here, because it's coming into my office."

Donna's plans for moving her coffin into her office are for a very aesthetic purpose. "We'll put it into my office. It's going to be a bookshelf where I need it. We double-utilize as much as we can," she says through an infectious laugh. "Who, but me, would be thinking like that?"

Maybe it's Donna's heritage in the interment business or raising eight children on the farm that has led to her holding such a pragmatic mantra: "Function before form, you know," she says with a chuckle.

"And I've already made arrangements to have my tombstone made. And it won't be conventional either; it will be flat. 'Cause I'm the cemetery sexton and I mowed that cemetery for eight years. You need to be able to run over it and not have to weed-eat around it. . . . And I've already got the stone picked out. I was raking the hay field, and I found the stone that I want. I just need to get help to get it out of there. You know, it's too heavy."

She knows her physical limitations, but Donna never is one to balk at a challenge. Her sharp mind and astute knowledge of the community's farming, family, and business needs led her to help pioneer the building of Marietta Kitchen Creations (MKC), a shared-use kitchen at the local fairgrounds in 2000. Donna and additional supporters of the project created the kitchen to help local growers prepare and preserve their own produce by commercially acceptable standards so they could sell their locally produced products to the consumers in their communities.

"We're trying to reinstitute a sense of community at the farming level," says Donna. "We meet with people who are interested in the project and find out their needs on a local level."

The resident farm dog keeps things on track and is shown "guarding" Donna's office.

This wood-burning furnace provides the heat on Donna's farm.

The fairground flooded in 2004 and the kitchen's facilities were devastated. But Donna didn't let a thing like that stop progress. She worked with her family and many others in the community to bring the equipment out to her farm's kitchen area. Her son Blayn helped finish and insulate one side of the large outbuilding near her house, and her daughter Denise went to Better Processing School and became licensed as a kitchen operator so she can officially teach others to use the equipment in the kitchen.

With the MKC added onto Gwamma's Farm kitchen, which was licensed in 2005, Donna and Denise now have the same contract with MKC as the fairgrounds had for the first few years. Donna hopes having the facility on her property might help her to better promote the kitchen and ensure its longevity.

Despite her best efforts, though, there remains a sense of political foreboding hanging over the small growers who want to bring their noncommercial food products to market. So far, the MKC allows members to can mostly tomato-based products. Donna says their range of prepared foods that can legally be preserved is very limited to acidic foods because the size of the group's existing equipment doesn't allow for enough pressure in the sealing process. The state's extension department offers a service that would help recalibrate the machines, but Donna has found out that the Ohio Department of Agriculture doesn't allow recalibration as a solution to its regulation standards.

Donna uses a golf cart to cruise around on her 200-acre farm.

The regulations leave almost no opportunity for MKC to increase its variety of foodstuffs—short of buying many thousands of dollars of new equipment. Donna is about as reserved in her opinion on this political Catch-22 as she is on most topics surrounding the agricultural industry, "They're trying to shut down the small producer in the favor of agribusiness," she states flatly. "You gotta get big or get out."

Her belief for the future of American food production and distribution is that eventually large agribusinesses will "control all of the food that's available in the United States." Donna laments the changes of today's national agriculture system because it leaves little room for sustainable community farming. "You know, these poverty pockets can't get big; there's no way we can get big."

Donna and the many other women in her area who practice organic and sustainable farming continue to fight the good fight and move forward with their limited-reach operations on a year-to-year basis. They wonder if the bureaucracy of agriculture in years to come will still allow them to sell the fruits of their labors off the family farm. Donna certainly has earned her stripes along the way, but she's not worried about tomorrow.

In the 40-plus years since the strong, independent young woman struck out to run her own family farm, Donna has witnessed her family grow through many changes. Donna, a soon-to-be great-great-grandmother, continues to face and overcome political and social challenges to her way of life and her way of farming. She looks back on times past as being just the stepping stones that have paved the way to the family farm life she has today—a very good life.

Like any farmer, Donna has faced many hardships, but she relies on her determination and strong will to keep moving forward.

Sarah Polyock
Chetek, Wisconsin

By Susan Gartner

"**J**ust thought you should know they get a little nervous with strangers and they might let loose," Sarah warns her guests who come into the barn as she milks the cows. And let loose they do. The photographer moves quickly to avoid getting splashed—and we're not talking milk here—but not quite quick enough. Healthy-looking with good muscle tone, straight teeth, and milky skin kissed by the Wisconsin sun, the cows are picture perfect—like something out of *Hoard's Dairyman: The National Dairy Farm Magazine*—and so is their owner, Sarah Polyock. She's even covered in the requisite dairy farmer dirt. "I'll be the filthiest farmer in your book!" Sarah tells the photographer.

Sarah is not a dairy farmer from way back. Her farm, located in Chetek, Wisconsin, 40 miles north of Eau Claire, wasn't passed down from her parents or grandparents and there are no fond mem-

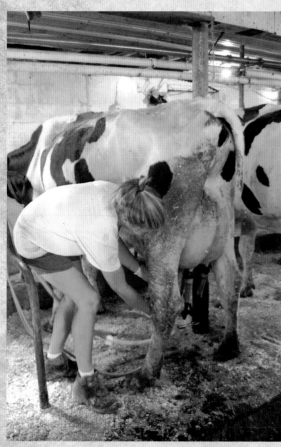

Sarah milks her 70 Holstein cows twice a day. She is a true early bird and starts every day at 3 a.m. on her farm in Chetek, Wisconsin.

OPPOSITE PAGE:
Sarah Polyock takes a minute out of her busy day to give some attention to one of her "coworkers," Rudy.

ories of milking cows as a child. "I milked my first cow when I was 19," she says. "Before that, I didn't have a clue."

After graduating from high school in her hometown of Lake Geneva, Wisconsin, where her dad was a grain farmer, Sarah went to school in Minneapolis to become a veterinarian technician. On weekends, she'd visit her brother Jake, who moved to Chetek in 1996 to be a dairy farmer. While there, she'd help him milk the cows. "He taught me how to do it and I liked it," she says, "and of course, I liked animals."

Although the days are long and full of work, Sarah absolutely loves her lifestyle. She is able to spend her days outside and surrounded by animals.

As her studies progressed, she had an internship at a vet clinic in Chetek. For six months, she lived with her brother and worked at the clinic. "After the internship," Sarah recalls, "the clinic offered me a full-time job and I took it. I'd milk for my brother in the evenings after work. After a year of that, my brother bought another herd of cows down the road."

To Sarah's surprise, she found herself thinking about her brother's farm the whole time she was working at the clinic. "I would wonder what the cows were doing, what was going on at that moment."

Jake asked her to quit her job and be full-time herd manager at the first farm while he managed the second. She did and it worked out great for six months. Then Jake decided he wanted to quit dairy farming, which left Sarah in a dilemma. "What am I supposed to do now?" she asked him. He convinced her to buy the cows from him. Through the Farm Service Agency (FSA), she was given a loan specifically for people like herself who don't have any equity or the kind of money on hand needed to make such a purchase.

"When I bought them in July 2000, I had 90 cows," Sarah says, "and I rented the facility from Jake. I would purchase all my feed from him. There were no employees. I did it all by myself." It's now 2006 and she is still managing the farm by herself.

"When I look back on that decision," Sarah tells me, "I wasn't scared, I wasn't nervous. I knew that's what I wanted to do. I didn't think about failing. I just knew this was the way I should go. Now I second-guess myself all the time!"

Her barn can house 55 cows. To milk 90, you have to milk the 55 cows, let them out of the barn, and then milk the remaining 35. "That was too much work," she sighs. During her second winter milking, she sold 25 cows. Now she's down to a more manageable 70 to 80 head.

To get a perspective on how much work is involved with a dairy farm, a typical husband-and-wife farm might have 40 cows with the husband and wife doing all the work. There's another unique twist to Sarah's situation. She lives three miles from the dairy farm. "I drive to work," she jokes.

"I get up before 3 a.m. to do basic chores. I bring the cows in the barn and start milking at 4 a.m. They get milked twice a day. I clean the cow yard [and] then feed the cows. I scrape down the barn, clean the mangers, and clean the gutter (the area behind where the cows stand that collects the manure). Then I check on and feed the dry cows. Those are cows that are due to have babies within two months. You stop milking them so they can get a break. Then there's usually something that needs to be fixed or needs to be cleaned. Or sometimes the vet is coming out."

Sarah isn't wistful about the turn her veterinary dream took. "I feel like I'm in an advantaged position because of my background," she says. "I can treat a lot of the animals myself. I'm good friends with my vet! It makes me realize that I am happy. No office politics at my farm!" she laughs.

At this point in the day, Sarah goes home for lunch or runs errands. Then she's back at the farm at 2:30 to feed the cows again. She brings them into the barn and

Sarah milked her first cow at 19 years old. Now 10 years later, she has her own herd that she's managed for the past 6 years.

After the cows are milked and grazing in the pasture, Sarah scrapes manure from the walk and stalls into the gutter.

milks them again at 4 p.m. "After milking, they go outside and I clean the barn again. It's pretty repetitive. Then I feed the calves. I typically get home around 7:30 or 8 at night. Maybe 9 or 10 if there's a problem like if there's a cow calving."

Sarah learned how to artificially inseminate the cows herself. "There's a man who comes and tells me which cow I should breed to which bull. For example, I might have a cow with bad feet but there's a bull that is known for producing good feet."

Sarah is proud of all that she's learned in just a few years. "I've learned so much about calving. I can put my arm in there and tell if I can do this on my own or if I need to call the vet. What amazes me about myself is I didn't know anything. I can remember watching the first cow ever have a baby and thinking, 'Why is this taking so long? Why is she doing that? What's that coming out?' And now I'm like, 'Duh.' I still

Sarah is teaching a calf to drink from a pail while a barn cat supervises.

get excited about it. Last month I had 20 cows calve. Next month, maybe I'll have two. Each cow has her own personality. They're not my pets, but I do care about them. I get excited wondering if it's going to be a girl or a boy and what it's going to look like."

The best part of being a dairy farmer for Sarah is working with the cows and being outside. "I get to be outside all the time, even when it's 20 below," she says happily. "When people ask me, 'Why do you work so hard?' I tell them when you like something, it doesn't seem like work. It doesn't feel like you're at your job. Dairy farming isn't a job. It's more like a lifestyle."

And the worst part of the job? "When it's 20 below!" she laughs. "The worst part of the job is when it's winter and you have three feet of snow and it's cold and the tractor

The cows turn a curious eye toward onlookers while they eat after the morning milking.

doesn't want to start and you have sick cows and the barn is frozen. I'm not real mechanical when it comes to fixing things, but I'm learning. I get thrown into situations where there's no one around to help me."

Sarah says her family is very supportive of her career. "My mom and dad live 300 miles from me, but my dad comes up a lot and changes oil for me. If something breaks down and it can wait, he'll come up and fix it. I've been lucky in that way. My parents worry about me because they see me working so hard. And I'm by myself most of the time. They worry if I were to get kicked by a cow and no one would be around to help me."

As for her brother, Jake, Sarah laughs at the irony of the situation. "Now he rents from *me!*" In April 2005, Sarah bought the 40 acres and the dairy barn and the house (that she rents out to someone else) from Jake. Their paths still cross daily. "He rents half the machine shed from me. He's in and out of the yard a lot. But we're two totally separate businesses." Jake does big square baling, farms 1,000 acres of his own with hay, plants corn, and puts up all of Sarah's corn silage. Sarah's other brother, Matt, took over their dad's crop farm in Lake Geneva. "My whole family is real proud of me,"

From the serene smile Sarah is always flashing, anyone can tell that she doesn't regret for one minute her career switch from a veterinary technician to a dairy farmer.

Sarah says. "Jake can't believe that I'm succeeding at this. A lot of people didn't think I'd last this long."

After the farm chores are finished, there's not much time left for anything else. Sometimes Sarah will go fishing, visit friends, or go to Lake Geneva to see her family. "I walk two miles every night," she says. "It helps me clear my head and unwind."

Sarah realizes her unique situation can cause some confusion. "I'm not from this area," she explains, "and it's hard to meet people when you're working alone all the time. When people come out to the farm they'll ask me, 'Is your dad around?' 'Is the boss home?' and I'll think, 'The boss of what?'"

What complicates matters is the difficulty of trying to take a vacation. "I'm not going to let the cows run my life," Sarah states. "You need a break, so you can come back rejuvenated. But you have to get someone to take over who is responsible. I don't know if I could do this forever. I can't be sick. I can't miss half a day. There's no one else. If I wake up and don't feel good, too bad. But luckily," she says with a glint in her eye, "I don't get sick 'cause I'm not around people!"

On the surface, Sarah's life has a peaceful, idyllic, unhurried routine with the cows and the cats and the two resident Rottweilers, Rallie and Rudy ("coworkers," she calls them), but there's a lot of stress underneath. "I know I can't keep this pace up forever," Sarah admits. "Right now, I'm not making money. I'm losing money every day. But luckily the last two years were really good and I have money to carry me through. Not enough people are aware of what dairy farmers get paid and the amount of work that they do. I don't have a lot of cash on hand, but I'm gaining equity."

Through it all, she remains optimistic about the future. "If I work really hard now and put my nose to the grindstone," Sarah projects, "maybe I'll be able to slow down later on and get hired help. If I ever did want to have a family, I couldn't do this on my own. I'm kind of a lost soul. My mother still asks me, 'What are you going to be when you grow up?' I'm just taking it day by day."

In the same way that the dairy farm first came to Sarah, she thinks a path will be revealed. "Someday something will happen," she says, attaching the milking unit to the cow, "and I'll think, 'This is the way I should go.'"

Eloise Stewart

Pinetta, Florida

By Susan Gartner

Eloise Stewart is a fourth-generation tree farmer, and at 95 years old, she still plays an active part in managing the farm.

OPPOSITE PAGE:
River View Farms, situated along the banks of the Withlacoochee River in Pinetta, Florida, has won awards and gained recognition for its environmental practices. None of the trees on the farm have ever been clear-cut.

The first thing you see when you approach the modest house is an ancient wrought-iron fence that is weathered with character and rich with detail. Mums and zinnias peek around rusty fence spikes that are topped with upside-down cast-iron acorns. A wooden sign that reads, "Welcome—C'mon in!" hangs on the fence and three tiny cowbells clang as the gate swings open.

Over 100 years ago, an ornate wrought-iron fence encircled the local cemetery where Eloise Stewart's ancestors are buried. In 1986, when overcrowding became a problem at the cemetery, the city tore the fence down. Eloise stepped in, salvaged what she could of the fence, and brought it home. The fence has seen a lot in its day. Folks have suggested that the fence should be repaired, repainted, and restored to its original condition. "I don't want it shiny and new," she tells them. "I like it the way it is."

Eloise Stewart is the matriarch of River View Farms, Inc., a tree farm located seven miles outside of Pinetta, Florida, on the Withlacoochee River, just south of the Georgia state line. Now 95 years old, Eloise spends most of her time gardening and rambling around the 1,000 acres of longleaf yellow pine that she collectively manages with her two daughters and "a very down-to-earth neighbor," who has rented the land for the past 10 years.

This rugged, rusty fence used to encircle the cemetery where Eloise's ancestors are buried. Eloise salvaged the gate when the cemetery was renovated and it is a true symbol of her sturdiness and devotion to her family and its history.

She's earned the right to ramble. Her daughters, Frances Copeland and Bennie Rose Stewart, are fifth-generation tree farmers. Unlike other farm women who do much of the physical labor themselves, the three women share an administrative role and oversee the management of thousands of acres. The land includes acreage that Eloise and her husband bought when they were first married and land she inherited from her parents. In addition to the trees, there has also been the management of cattle, pigs, chickens, and roosters. They've been farming for a long time and do it well. River View Farms has the reputation for being one of the best managed tree farms in all of Florida. It has also gathered recognition and awards for its environmentally sensitive practices.

For readers familiar with the practice of raising cattle, corn, or kids, but out of the loop when it comes to raising trees, there is definitely a skill involved. "With tree farming," Phil Gornicki, director of Responsible Forestry at the Florida Forestry Association explains, "you have to remove competing vegetation and weeds so young seedlings have a chance to grow. Harvesting trees selectively creates little clearings. The trees drop their seeds and you have seedlings come in naturally." This winning formula, known as select-cutting, was passed down to Eloise.

Other tree-farming companies choose to clear-cut, which is felling and removing all trees in a designated area in one operation. Clear-cutting and select-cutting methods have their pros and cons. "Granddaddy and Father didn't like the idea of clear-cutting," Frances, 67, says. "They would watch various companies come into an area and cut all the trees down, then put in new trees with herbicides."

If Eloise's father and husband were alive today, the two men might have appreciated being at the forefront of a major controversy as pro-environmental organizations hold clear-cutting practices responsible for soil erosion, habitat loss, and the elimination of fish and wildlife.

"Clear-cutting is okay in many circumstances," Phil says. "Most commercial pines do not grow well in shade. If you were to remove 40 acres through clear-cutting and replant, you will get your fastest growth response because the young seedlings will have the benefit of full sun. Select-cutting takes more skill and patience to make it work. The landowner has to be willing to accept a slower growth of seedlings. They're competing with the adult trees for light, nutrients, and water. It takes longer to get those young trees up to a commercially valuable size."

Bennie Rose, 64, is quick to point out the benefits of their system. "Our trees have never been clear-cut," she proudly states. "We pick and choose the trees we want to cut, then sell that timber. Generations can come and see trees in their natural habitat. The trees go in cycles. The big trees plant small trees. As they become big trees, they are cut to allow the smaller trees to grow. The cycle goes on generation after generation."

The logistics of getting equipment and trucks through a densely forested area to fell certain trees without disturbing other trees can be complicated. Clear-cutting is infinitely easier and much less expensive. Select-cutting requires more finesse, time, and more money. Eloise and her daughters feel the environmental benefits outweigh any logistical challenges.

"We have designated roads through these woods," Bennie Rose says. "When you come in and select-cut, you're not going all over the property. One of the reasons our farm doesn't clear-cut is because of our love of nature and the earth. These trees help clean our air and we're committed to maintaining a balance of nature. We like the fact that the animals are not disturbed."

Another aspect of tree farming that takes patience and consideration is prescribed burning. These are low-temperature fires deliberately set under highly controlled circumstances that take into account weather conditions, fire breaks (paths designed to keep the fire contained within a certain area), and the people and equipment needed to keep things under control.

Eloise learned how to run a farm by working with her grandfather, father, and husband. When her husband had a stroke in 1970, Eloise didn't miss a beat, and she took over managing the farm.

This hunting lodge was built in 1982 to replace the original that had hosted many domestic and foreign government leaders visiting with the Pepsi Cola Company. Today the lodge is only used by the family.

"You need to remove decaying vegetation so it doesn't build up too much on the forest floor," Phil explains. "If you do this periodically under controlled conditions, you almost eliminate the possibility of a catastrophic fire. Putting a prescribed fire in an area every 3 or 5 years removes the competing vegetation and allows the pines to dominate the site. If you burn when the trees are too small, you will burn them up. When they get a little bigger, their bark is thick enough to where a low-temperature fire will not do damage to the pine. If you know what you're doing, the fire will stimulate the growth of certain herbs that wildlife eat and keep the land open for turkeys and quail."

It's the quail that got the two daughters involved in the first place. "We wouldn't have learned how to do this if it wasn't for our daddy," says Bennie Rose. "He started this because he loved to quail hunt. He wanted a natural place for the quail." The 1,000 acres of natural wiregrass and towering longleaf pine made the perfect setting for the Madison Hunting Club, an offshoot venture that was a direct result of the timber business. Back in the mid-1960s, the property was leased to the Pepsi Cola Company for hunting purposes, which attracted many important U.S., foreign, and government business leaders. Jeeps and bird dogs had to be purchased, special hunting guides had to be trained, along with securing the key ingredient to the whole operation—quail eggs! Eloise and the farm cook, Suzie Mae, prepared gourmet southern dishes for world leaders in the old country kitchen of a rustic, Civil War-era two-story lodge. Unfortunately, the lodge burned down and a new lodge was built in 1982 on the Withlacoochee River. No longer used for commercial hunting purposes, this lodge is now enjoyed by equally important visiting dignitaries—Eloise's grandchildren.

A herd of beef cattle also reside on the River View Farms.

This legacy of care toward conservation yields a high-quality timber that can be sold and made into lumber, plywood, and telephone poles. "Longleaf pine is commonly used for that [making telephone poles]," Phil confirms. "It grows very straight and has a good form class, meaning the trunk doesn't taper much. Longleaf grows cylindrical, so in any given tree you get more solid wood products from it. You want lots of useable wood all the way to the top of the tree." When Eloise's father ran the business, he had customers in Africa. "I remember Poppa carrying the timber to the railroad and loading it onto boxcars," recalls Eloise. She still has the original telegram with the order.

"We have a pine forest that is very unique," Frances says. The Florida Division of Forestry has awarded the property certification as part of the Forest Stewardship Program. Because of this certification, forestry staff will bring in guests to tour River View Farms and hold up their conservation practices as an ideal model.

In order to run such an ideal farm, one needs to have a strong will, knowledge, and intuition. Eloise has all of these qualities and then some, which is monumental considering she had a rough start. Eloise wasn't expected to survive childhood. She was five years old when she contracted typhoid fever, and it took her three years to recover. It wasn't until she was nine years old that she was well enough to start school. It was a situation that really didn't work out so badly. School only lasted six months out of the year back then, and children often didn't start until they were eight years old. Although she was late to graduate, Eloise wasn't far behind her peers. It didn't affect her socializing skills—her playmates were often the children who worked in the fields.

In 1932, Eloise married Lewis Stewart who, at the time, was part-owner of his family's grocery store. Lewis wanted to get out of the family business and into a business of his own. When 1,000 acres came up for sale during the Depression, Lewis didn't know anything about farming but he knew a good deal when he saw one—land priced at $3.50 an acre! With the help of five families who also lived on the farm, the couple restored the land and an old farmhouse that was built in 1870 for their future family.

Frances remembers a childhood filled with cotton, corn, cattle, watermelon, birthing calves, harvesting tobacco, and early entrepreneurial adventures. "My granddaddy would give me a pig every year and I'd feed it with a bottle and keep it around until it got bigger. Then I'd make my dad give me money for the pig," Frances laughs.

Bennie Rose remembers churning butter that her mother would sell in town. "She would cook lunch for the people who worked on the farm," Bennie Rose recalls. "After a hog or chicken or cow was slaughtered, it was her job to see that the meat was salted and smoked in the smokehouse. After vegetables were picked, she would can and freeze them so we would have food during the winter months." While everyone was working on the farm, if a truck or piece of machinery broke down, Eloise was the one who went into town to get the right part. In addition to her vegetable, meat, and mechanical responsibilities, she also looked after and nurtured all the humans.

This old shanty was home to workers on the farm.

When the baby of a worker suddenly died, Eloise made a proper burial gown out of a white curtain.

"Momma used to send us out to get sugar or other supplies for the workers," recalls Bennie Rose, "and we'd go down and bring it to their house and we'd come back and Momma would say, 'Why have you been gone so long?' I'd reply, 'Well, I had supper with them!'"

For 38 years, the family worked the land to a profitable state. While her husband worked in the field alongside the field hands, Eloise was "farming from my kitchen window." Then in 1970, Lewis suffered a stroke. He didn't lose any of his mental capacities, but he could no longer manage the physical aspects of farming.

"Right after the stroke, Momma took over everything for awhile," says Bennie Rose. "She amazed me because she helped so many people in the last moments of their lives. She has seen five or six family members pass. I think her having to help other people like that made her realize a little more about what somebody goes through. I think it made her more compassionate towards Daddy and more determined to help him through it. She wouldn't let him give up. She kept pushing. He began to get a little better and tried to show a little more interest. I admired her for trying to keep him involved. It took a lot of patience on her part."

Eloise's farm and forestry savvy came by way of a long apprenticeship, first through her grandfather and father, and then through her husband. By the time Lewis died in 1988, the management of the farm had completely shifted to Eloise. Unfortunately, the stress took its toll on the family. "She turned away from her daughters after he died," recalls Bennie Rose. "She wouldn't let us in. She wouldn't let us help."

Frances, Eloise, and Bennie Rose pose for a picture on the banks of the Withlacoochee River.

In 1990, Eloise was diagnosed with breast cancer. After a radical mastectomy, chemotherapy, and radiation treatments, she is now cancer-free. "My doctor is as happy about this as I am!" laughs Eloise.

After Eloise inherited property from her father in 1979, she began to develop a subdivision on her own. "She just went to the courts and got it started," Bennie Rose says proudly about her mother. "In 2000, she deeded it over to Frances and me. It forced my sister and I to work together. Forced us to communicate on a business level. We now have mutual respect for each other. It's the best thing our Momma ever did for us. Momma saw how we could work together in a peaceful atmosphere in a joint direction and we're successful at making this happen. I really think that parents are there to guide, and not control. Mother stayed out of it and let us do whatever we wanted to do. She just stood back and watched us. Because of this, she saw we were very capable women. Very business-oriented. We know how to get things done. She learned how to appreciate a part of us that she wouldn't have seen if she hadn't given us the property. It bonded all three of us in a way that wouldn't have happened otherwise."

Eloise has also deeded property to her grandchildren. "She's tried to maintain the family heritage and awareness of the next generation having ownership in what Great-granddaddy had left to her," explains Frances. All five grandchildren currently maintain the property given to them by their grandmother in hopes to continue this family tradition.

At the time of this writing, there are 80 acres of yellow pine being planted on River View Farms. These trees won't be ready to be sold for lumber for 25 years. In our instant-messaging, microwave-paced society, it takes a certain patience to appreciate that form of progress and that kind of beauty.

The regeneration of Eloise Stewart's family reveals itself in the cycle of the trees. The seedlings fall on the soft forest floor, get nurtured by the surrounding trees, put down roots, grow straight and grow tall, and reach for the sun.

Laura Adams
Cedar Key, Florida

By Bethany Weaver-Culpepper

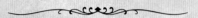

Laura Adams shows off the product of her hard work and patience.

OPPOSITE PAGE:
Laura is shown sorting the clams by size.

"Strange coincidences" are the words Laura Adams uses to describe how she ended up in Cedar Key, Florida. Once a tiny gulf island that was home to shipping, trading, and fishing, Laura discovered a community that many flock to for its artisan works and outlying resort areas. At the turn of the century, the major industries left the island and challenged the community to find a niche. Since Cedar Key is less than an hour from Gainesville, tourists eventually rediscovered the Gulf of Mexico island. Laura did not start her journey to Florida as a tourist, nor as her current profession, a clam farmer. Laura came to Florida with dreams of owning her own restaurant. But dreams are not often what they seem, and they can end up leading in a direction that is entirely different from what we had originally expected.

Laura grew up on a 50-acre farm in Connecticut, and she was the second child of five. She moved to the city, went to college, and received a degree in social services. Yet, after working a year and a half as a social worker, Laura realized the job was too heartbreaking. That's when she went into the restaurant business and became a bartender. Around this time Laura married and had her first two children, a son and daughter. A few years later, Laura divorced her husband and later met a chef who is her younger daughter's father.

Full-sized clams are run through a tumbler to help in the sorting process.

With a strong desire to leave behind local committee boards and the frantic city life, both Laura and her partner dreamed of opening their own restaurant. With the money she made from selling her Connecticut home, Laura ventured to Florida with her family in tow to discover the perfect place to start a new business. She and her family drove to the Gulf Coast and looked for a new place to settle in many different towns, yet they had skipped over Cedar Key because Laura heard there was not much there. Before she purchased the ideal restaurant, Laura felt she should at least drive through Cedar Key to see what it had to offer. There may not have been much there in the modern way of living, but when Laura arrived, she knew she had found her home in the small town of 1,000 people.

Laura ran her own restaurant for three years until she decided that enough was enough. In the restaurant business, Laura says, "You either get hard workers or you don't." Although she had some good employees throughout those years, she worked very long hours. On the recommendation of a friend, she kept track of how many hours she put in over the course of a week. Laura was shocked to find she worked a whopping 94 hours each week. Needless to say, she realized this dream was no longer what she wanted. She told photographer Cathy Phillips, "There's not a Sunday that I don't wake up and thank God I don't have a restaurant anymore." Today she has what restaurants need and what wholesalers buy from her—clams.

Laura came to Cedar Key in 1995, which was the same year the net ban was implemented. This law made it illegal for both commercial and sporting fisherman to use nets for fishing. It was devastating to fishing families who had made their incomes off the water. The state of Florida came in to help and created a program for people to farm-raise clams. A farmer would buy a land lease for $25 and then were taught how to farm-raise clams on that land.

"Cedar Key has a lot of food in the water. The clams grow beautiful," Laura proudly stated. Her clams grow in about half the time it may take a South Carolinian clam farmer.

By the time Laura left the restaurant business in 1998, the lease price for land to farm-raise clams had substantially risen to $25,000 for a leased two acres of land. Before she decided to purchase a lease, she worked for a large clamming company to see if she wanted to become a clam farmer. Her job at the company was to turn clam bags inside out. When an employee left, she transferred to the position of seeding clams.

Laura sorts her clams as they fall out of the tumbler.

There are different ways to grow clams. Laura farms in the open Gulf water and prefers to start from seed, which is the size of a salt grain. Laura feels that if you start with seed, you know what you're getting. Some farmers prefer to start with nursery bags of baby clams. Laura explains that a baby clam is about the size of your pinky fingernail.

Seeding is Laura's favorite part about clam farming. She loves the seeds and compares caring for them to the way you would a child or pet. "You have to keep them clean. They like to be bunched together when they are small, but as they grow, you need to give them room." Laura plants about 3 million baby seeds per year and begins her planting in March. After the seeds have been planted for 15 months, they are large enough to pick.

When the baby clams are this size, they are placed into bags on the bed of the Gulf of Mexico to grow to full size.

Laura has about a 60 percent success rate and with the larger clams, she may have a 75 to 80 percent success rate. As with any type of farming, some years she has had a yield as low as 30 percent and it is hard to recover from a slow year. Laura said between the effect on the economy due to September 11, 2001, and four hurricanes that killed the crop, she has not been able to fully catch up. It is difficult when what you plant and harvest doesn't come to fruition. Yet, that is the way it is with the life of a farmer, whether you're working on land or in the water.

Summer is the busiest time of the year for clamming. Laura's day begins at 6:30 a.m. with the morning tide. Laura stated, "The early tides give clams a better shelf life." When asked if she was able to read the weather when she went to Florida or if someone taught her about the moon and tides, Laura explains, "Everyone will tell you something about the tides." After farming for a few years, she has learned what the tides mean for her clams and her work. Laura feels that even though being a farmer means always being busy—whether it is seeding, pulling, doing paperwork, or cleaning the chicken wire from the lease—"Life is so calm." Clam farming is not just an income, it is a way of life.

Laura is a fast talker and her open, friendly nature portrays a woman who is willing to do whatever needs to be done. Farming has brought out a competitive side of Laura. "I have a hard time with something not being fair," Laura reveals. People either love her or hate her. Her strong work ethic is something that has been passed along to her children. Her son, Jordan, shares the workload with his mom. His name is on the lease with Laura and he is truly her right-hand man. "Jordan loves to farm," adds Laura. She has learned to trust her son's instinct and relies on him when making decisions. "When I don't know what to do or how to handle a situation, I think, 'What would Jordan do?' It usually works out, which is a testament to Jordan's excellent farming and business skills. Because Laura does not hire help, Jordan and the family are her team. There are always nursery bags that need to be patched, as well as raceways and tumblers that need attention. On a yearly basis, Laura and her youngest daughter clean the rusty chicken wire that they lay over the land to keep predators at bay.

Summer is the busiest time of year for Laura because she is busy picking and sorting clams.

Laura grows and sells her clams to farmers. She also sells to two wholesalers in town. She explained that the business side of farming is still an adjustment. Her clients may pay on a regular basis for weeks, and then skip a week. That is when her son tells her, "Go down there and get the check." She does not feel this has anything to do with who she is as a person, but it's simply a business where you have to be on your toes.

As one of the two female clam farmers in Cedar Key, she has found nothing but respect between men and women farmers. If there is any discrimination toward female farmers, she does not feel it. In fact, in the beginning she noticed that Jordan expected

CLOSED
FARM RAISED CLAMS
SHRIMP
MULLET
OYSTERS
NO SMOKING
SEAFOOD
MARKET

Laura rakes the baby clams in the nursery.

PREVIOUS PAGE;
As she stands outside a market that sells her clams, Laura is an example of the resilient and determined spirit embodied by all farmers.

her to do just as much heavy lifting as he did., Now they have everything worked out and are a good team. Jordan may pull a 100-pound bag of clams, while she is taking care of the paperwork. As far as the other male farmers in Cedar Key, she lightheartily stated, "I feel I've earned their respect, or they just can't stand me."

You can tell not only by her words, but by the tone in her voice, that Laura loves living in Cedar Key. She is proud of her hard work and accomplishments as a clam farmer. She loves the strong, mud smell and watching the porpoises, manatees, and green sea turtles, but the beauty is not keeping Cedar Key regulars from moving off the island. Prices for homes in the area are high and although she tries to stay open-minded, she worries that the new people moving into Cedar Key are "selling their way of life." The residents who are moving into town don't have children, and she worries that their small school system of 200 students may not have the necessary funding someday. She loves their schools, but admits some partiality because her oldest daughter is the language arts teacher and also happens to teach Laura's youngest daughter. By the sounds of it, Laura's family is full of independent women. Her youngest daughter helped run her dad's ice cream shop and saved up enough money to buy a herself a laptop and a bicycle that was given to Laura for Mother's Day.

Although Laura is very proud of clamming, she shines even brighter while talking about her children. She is single and believes being a single parent may be easier. She does not regret any aspect of her life. She confidently proclaims, "I never look back," and that goes for most things in her life. Laura explains that she and the kids, "did not have anything to fall back on except for each other." That bond cannot be broken and is something that is strengthened daily. Every night, she cooks a meal and sits down with her children for dinner. Laura loves to spend money on good food and she buys a lot of groceries. She enjoys the family time that comes from the nightly dinners. Laughing, she says that if she needs to find her son, people just tell her to turn the grill on—that'll bring him home.

Laura has called Cedar Key home for 11 years and says it's the longest she has lived anywhere since being a kid on the farm. Laura chuckles and says that her goal someday is to find something to occupy her time when her kids are gone. "Maybe I'll be a Louisiana catfish farmer." Her independent nature does not stop her from slowing down to have some fun. She is involved in many family activities. They go boating and enjoy rope swinging into the river near her son's home. "There are alligators in the river, but they leave us alone." It took her youngest daughter some time to feel safe, but now they all go and have a great time. One of her favorite things to do is sit around the campfire with her family and a guitar to talk and sing.

Laura wants to keep clam farming for as long as possible. She wants her family to remember this time in her life as something that was full of hard work, but something that she loved. Philosophically, Laura states, "You have to remember, you're at the mercy of something you can't control and most people can't handle that. It's farming. You have to be square with that." By the confident tone in her voice, you can tell she is square with that. She is proud of her seeds and loves watching them grow into the clams that support her calm way of life. Jordan will continue to farm after Laura decides to move on or retire, whichever comes first, though she says that retirement scares her. Like many farmers, she does not have much saved up for retirement but that does not stop her from living this simple lifestyle she has made her own.

Net Ban

Approved by voter referendum in November 1994, Amendment Three, also referred to as the net ban, made the use of entangling nets in Florida water unlawful. This practice and its results have caused a continuous debate between commercial and sporting fisherman. For some, there has been growth due to net ban; however, for many fisherman there has been a substantial loss.

According to the article, "What Happened After the Net Ban" by Chuck Adams, Steve Jacobs, and Suzanne Smith, "When comparing the two time periods, three-quarters of the families interviewed remained in fishing following the net ban. The percentage of fishers fishing full-time dropped from 90 percent at Time 1 to 70 percent at Time 2. About one-quarter of the fishers interviewed had retired from commercial fishing entirely. Of those still fishing, 70 percent continue to fish full-time.

"The percentage of family income from fishing was reduced from 80 percent to 55 percent following the net ban. These families reported becoming far more dependent on non-fishing sources of income. The additional nonfishing income sources were primarily contributed by wives. However, husbands' nonfishing paid work doubled from an average of 6 hours at Time 1 to 12 hours per week at Time 2."

Although Florida spent millions of dollars on several assistance programs, most programs failed to help families for a variety of reasons. The benefits of the ban may be seen as stocks of fin fish continue to improve.

Rose Koenig

Gainesville, Florida

By Holly L. Bollinger

These freshly harvested eggplant are bound for a farmers' market.

Imagine for a minute what it would take to plan, plant, feed, weed, and harvest a garden large enough to satisfy your family with fresh, pesticide-free produce for at least 32 weeks each year. Now, add another 93 hungry families into the equation with enough weekly surpluses to sell at outdoor markets in three counties. Oh, and don't forget to reserve some of your time and effort to devote to the 20-plus varieties of fresh-cut flowers you'll be arranging and selling as bouquets to your vendors. Now, pack it all onto just 17 acres of a sandy, subtropical patch of suburbia—it's an awesome site. For all of those who've tasted its fruit, it's an organic paradise. For one Yankee-born Garden State transplant to north central Florida, it's simply a way of life.

Rose Koenig, owner and operator of Rosie's Organic Farm, has worked an average of 14-hour days for more than a decade. Rose's farm is located just outside the shadow of Gainesville's fast-growing urban sprawl. Organic farm life is especially challenging during peak season when her days overflow with a mix of bountiful harvests, painstaking preparations for the next group of plantings, and weekly marketing efforts that take her and her family as far north up the coast as Amelia's Island near the border of Georgia.

"Originally, I was doing it just seasonally," Rose says with a laugh in regard to the humble beginnings of her unique farm in 1993. "I started it as part-time, supplementing

Rose gives customers at the farmers' market samples of cantaloupe grown at her farm.

my graduate student stipend." But after the birth of her daughter in 1995, the then-doctorate student in plant pathology was in full swing of writing her dissertation and running the farm. She and her husband, Tom, decided she could take on the farming full-time and reevaluate the job situation after their children were in elementary school. The short-term projection of a farm for a few years turned into a long-term success for many in the community.

Rose is the daughter of a generational farmer who had inherited his New Jersey-based vegetable and chicken operation from his parents. "My father was a pretty traditional farmer," Rose reminisces. "He was born in 1917, so he really was farming prior to the chemical revolution in agriculture."

Although it is an organic approach by today's standards, at the time Rose's dad farmed, the only way to reap the benefits of fertilizer was to use the science of nitrogen-fixing ground cover and the manure from the family's layer hens. "So it was by default; it really wasn't a conscious issue. It was just the way he farmed, with his cover crops and such. So that wasn't foreign to me."

Rose took her first-hand farming knowledge and experiences with her to Rutgers University, where she earned her Bachelor of Science in Agriculture Science from the Cook College. In college, Rose's hold on modern agricultural issues and her feelings about the importance of sustainable farming deepened. She moved out west to earn her master's degree in International Agricultural Development from the University of California, Davis. While living in California, friends introduced her to the state's progressive "organic movement" in the early days of standardized organic certification for growers.

Then Rose went to work in Africa with the Rodale Institute, a 60-year-old organization founded on the scientific philosophy of "Healthy Soil = Healthy Food = Healthy People." At that point, she knew her knowledge and the efforts of her group from the U.S. would help the local farmers apply better practices to their long-held traditional farming beliefs. But Rose does like to emphasize the difference between the ideals of improving traditional farming and organic farming.

"That was real traditional, without really mechanization even," Rose says. "The project in Africa dealt with cover crops and low input systems, which, again, is sort of low-input by default because folks there just don't have money to put into their systems. I like to call them more traditional systems, because to me, organic is more of a management regime. I don't use it. It's really trying to actively figure out how to manage a system through different techniques, [it requires] a different knowledge base than just doing it traditionally because you don't have access to something."

Following her work in Africa, Rose came stateside to begin her Ph.D in Plant Pathology at the University of Florida. She moved to Gainesville to complete her doctorate work and she wanted the subtropical focus. "At that time, my husband and I were planning to go back overseas to work, but we needed a home base," she explains.

"As I was going though my degree program, I really felt like I was getting further away from agriculture and more into the laboratory. So I kind of actually started the operation to balance the work that I was doing for my PhD."

Rose began farming on the 10 acres she and Tom own in the suburbs. Right from the beginning, Rose knew she would need to find markets for her products to earn the money she needed to keep her farm and her organic progressions afloat.

"I immediately became certified in organics. I wanted to at least try," she says. "A lot of people told me it wasn't possible to do in Florida, but I figured I might as well try it. You can always try it and then go to conventional, but once you start conventional it's too hard to try to go organic."

Rose supposes that because of Florida's size, the state's focus tends to lean toward large-scale agriculture and transporting most products in large out-of-state shipments. "These large farms are really intensively growing and also have a pretty high use of pesticide applications," she says. "They're kind of into the spray paradigm."

Despite the little understanding by the agricultural establishment at the universities she dealt with, Rose wasn't deterred from her goal to grow and sell organic. "I had witnessed it in New Jersey; I couldn't see why it couldn't happen in Florida, contrary to what the experts were saying."

Rose's path was paved with determination, but that didn't make it a smooth ride. "As far as the marketing goes, in Gainesville when we started in 1993, there was only one retail establishment, one farmers' market that the county had established in conjunction with farmers," she says in reference to the Alachua County Farmers' Market. "We started there, but it was not a very progressive market.

"They didn't allow really any value-added types of products," she explains, "any kind of processed foods. I had come from California where the markets were just a mixture of food products, not only just raw fruits and vegetables," she says in reference to jams and other processed derivatives of the organic ingredients. "The rules were flexible to allow—I guess—to be more proconsumer. Here that concept was more like a religion that 'It could only be raw fruits and vegetables.'"

Rose stayed with the market for the next few years, meanwhile working with additional growers in the area who held her similar interests in branching out and starting more progressive farmers' market opportunities. They decided it was too much of an upset to try to change the existing retail outlet. "We just decided to create our own and figured that the best way to change things is by showing by another example."

The collective effort by local growers led to the opening of the Union Street Farmers' Market in downtown Gainesville in the mid-1990s. Community Green Markets of North Florida Inc. is the nonprofit organization, founded by Rose and four

Rose tends to the plants and does most of the fieldwork on her own, although she does have many volunteers who love to help.

Rose's children are very involved with the farm and assist in the fields and at farmers' markets.

other growers as an umbrella organization. Soon after, the group was able to establish another popular farmers' market, named for the large subdivision it borders, the Haile Plantation, to which Rose is still the primary marketing contact. Through years of word-of-mouth endorsements and happy customers, Rose and her peers have found markets that reach beyond the local comforts of her new hometown.

Today, many times during each season (lasting from November to mid-June), Rose's family packs up their fresh pickings to head for a two-hour Saturday drive up the coast to the Fernandina Farmers' Market on Amelia Island, near the Georgia border. For Rose, the new market means new consumer tastes and fresh crowds for her organic products. "The community there is real supportive. Similar to other [states], it's difficult to always find enough farmers for these local farmers' markets."

Although Rose still welcomes the home market crowd, and the biggest volume of produce moves at her mainstay Haile Plantation Market, she acknowledges that different venues bring a variety of consumers that's not always predictable. "Every market crowd has different preferences. A lot of it is just education over time. At the markets here in Gainesville, we've got a lot of educated consumers because over the years, people have tried a lot of vegetables and they eat a wide variety of stuff.

"In Fernandina Beach, it's a newer market, so we grow a lot of stuff that you can't find in the local supermarket. So over time, I think their preferences there will change. But right now, it's not what I would call the meat-and-potatoes, but it's the potatoes-bean-and-broccoli market."

The biggest achievement to blossom out of Rosie's Farm isn't the throngs of loyal customers who traverse northern Florida to find the organic stands at weekly outdoor markets. It's the families of people who depend on her growing success for their own families' major nutrition source. In 1996, Rose agreed to be the farm host for the second Floridian Community Supported Agriculture (CSA) project, which came to fruition due to one couple's own marketing efforts in her community. "They had been following the CSA movement around the country and they were trying to get something started in Florida. At that time there was only one CSA in Tampa, and that was it for the whole state of Florida.

"I heard of them, and I heard that they were trying to do this," says Rose about the couple's efforts trying to recruit a local farmer to participate. What the couple needed was a farmer who would agree to sell shares of the annual crop to meet their family needs for certain fresh fruits and vegetables or flowers. The family buys a share of Rose's annual produce selection, and they can collect on a weekly basis at either the local farmers' markets or at the farm on those same designated days.

Rose finally met the couple in central Florida during a public speaking engagement. The couple brought a list of customer recruits who were on board with the CSA concept. "They told me how they were interested and actually already had a list of consumers that were ready to sign up," Rose says. "At that time, I wasn't sure that I would be interested in buying a CSA share if I was a consumer. But then, I thought, 'That's just me. Why would I deny a set group of consumers access? Plus, they're going to pay,' so I thought I might as well try it."

Rose's first year as the Plowshares CSA farmer networked 35 shareholder families. It was a big step away from the mostly wholesale business that Rose had built during the previous few years, but she welcomed the change. "My goal always had been to try to do as much retail as possible, so I really saw it as an avenue of doing more retail and something in addition to the farmers' market," she says. "We just celebrated our 10th year, and now we have about 93 families locally."

Her marketing strategy is simple: Rose relies on happy customers to spread the word across the state, as far away as Jacksonville. "A lot of people in the state ask us, 'How far do you deliver?' And locally, it's just really blossomed on its own because we don't really do any advertising other than word of mouth."

Rose only puts in shares of what she grows on her farm. If her farm doesn't provide a certain product, she encourages her shareholders to buy that product from another farmer at the farmers' market.

Along with many varieties of fruits and vegetables, Rose sells flowers at the farmers' market.

Plowshares CSA shareholder members can also choose to participate in the community's Share the Harvest effort where members donate portions of the shares or sponsor additional shares for needy and low-income families in the area. For every sponsored share, Rose matches with an equal amount from her own interest.

The more the shareholders get involved with Rosie's Farm, the more they uphold the true spirit of community-supported farming. Although Rose does most of the day-to-day fieldwork, she welcomes the help of community volunteers and frequently hires interns from the university to learn the inner workings of an organic operation.

With or without the help of additional hands, Rose has a lot of work to do every day, from the fall planting's greenhouse seedlings that are started in late August to final harvests and sales in mid-June. "We have a long season here. You could theoretically grow year-round," says Rose, but she reserves a block of free time each year during the summer months for her most important commitment—her family.

Rose's CSA shareholders benefit from the longer growing seasons by getting about eight months of fresh produce, compared with only an average of five or six months at the most in other CSA states.

Rose grows more than 40 types of organic fruits and vegetables and more than 20 varieties of flowers for the profitable fresh-cut market. She says she usually keeps the popular produce as staples in her year-to-year growing plan, including mainstream

Through Rose's hard work and determination, 93 families have shares in her farm.

vegetables, such as broccoli, zucchini, squash varieties, lettuce, cucumbers, tomatoes, sweet corn, and eggplant. The other products vary depending on customer preferences. For instance, it's not uncommon that Rose will grow several varieties of Asian greens. "Through trial-and-error, after doing it for 13 years, you kind of figure out what works for you and what doesn't."

Although the list of crops she planted a decade ago might have been a little longer than today, Rose quickly weeded out the less desirable items in favor of the more popular sellers. Brussels sprouts didn't make the cut, along with some of the bitters, such as dandelion greens and Italian greens.

Rose plows ahead and month after month she provides her shareholders, less-fortunate neighbors, customers, vendors, and her family with many of the common vegetables and a diverse group of the unusual varieties they crave, "But there are only so many bok choys that you can sell," she muses.

On a more serious note, Rose imparts how important the aspect of her relationship with the community is to her decision-making in organic farming. "Those are the kinds of things you just learn by really being involved in the operation on a day-to-day basis and knowing what your customers want and going to the farmers' markets," says Rose.

"I pretty much do it all, from choosing what to grow to harvesting to selling to interacting with customers. And by doing that, I think you can have a good gauge on your consumer."

Rose's work with the CSA and farmers' markets are ways she is helping to reconnect the consumers with the farmers.

A World of Community

The Community Supported Agriculture (CSA) idea isn't a new concept. Since the mid-1980s, hundreds of CSA farms have been founded worldwide. Although it has only recently caught on across the state of Florida, which now has eight CSA groups similar to the Plowshares CSA, similar efforts are much more wide-sweeping in other states such as New York, California, and Wisconsin. According to Rose Koenig, owner and operator of Rosie's Farm in Gainesville, Florida, "They've got festivals where consumers come and choose which CSA they want to join."

Wikipedia, a popular Internet-based encyclopedia resource, defines the CSA movement as, "a relatively new socio-economic model of food production, sales, and distribution aimed at both increasing the quality of food and the quality of care given the land, plants, and animals, while substantially reducing potential food losses and financial risks for the producers. It is also a method for small-scale commercial farmers and gardeners to have a successful, small-scale closed market. CSAs focus usually on a system of weekly delivery or pick-up of vegetables, sometimes also flowers, fruits, herbs, and even milk or meat products in some cases. A variety of production and economic sub-systems are in use worldwide."

According to Rose and the other founders of the Plowshares CSA that her farm supplies, the basis for such a relationship between the members and the farmer fulfills as much the social needs of the community as it meets the economic situations and physical demands of the consumers. The PlowsharesCSA.org web site reads, "Community-supported agriculture is an international movement that is providing people with an alternative to the global food system. Many hundreds of CSAs have formed in the U.S. alone since 1985. The movement arose as a local and human scale response to the worldwide damage to farmers, farm communities, and the environment which has occurred with large scale conventional agriculture.

"Small farmers everywhere are faced with leaving the land because of low food prices. The movement seeks to restore direct contact between farmers and consumers."

Jessica Norfleet

Newberry, Florida

By Susan Gartner

Jessica and her husband, Paul, are constantly busy with their animals, watermelons, and contracting business, but it is a busy life full of many rewards.

OPPOSITE PAGE:
Jessica's love of horses goes back to her childhood, and she still spends any spare time on horseback.

Jessica Norfleet's workspace could certainly pass for a typical corporate cubicle. The two office chairs are firm but cushy with good neck and back support; they are upholstered in a stain-resistant, blue-grey tweed that matches the carpet. The room temperature is easily maintained and can be adjusted to her personal preference with the flick of a dial. Better than a corner office, the expansive windows open and close at the push of a button and offer a 360-degree view of the world.

You can almost envision her sitting at an executive desk to negotiate a contract on a cell phone, with her pearl earrings peeking out from under auburn hair she has pulled back in a casual ponytail. She'd fit right in at any corporate office if it weren't for that pesky steering wheel, console, and glove compartment running through the middle of it all. Half a dozen building plans are rolled up on the dashboard of her 2004 Chevy 4x4 pickup, along with the day's mail. Two manila folders rest on the middle cushion of the front seat. The folders are stuffed with construction job contracts and correspondence between municipalities, contractors, vendors, and inspectors. On top of that stack sits a thick, black planner that is bulging with notes and appointment reminders. A purse, lunch bag, and water bottle rest on the center hump of the truck floor next to a 12-gauge and a 20-gauge pump action shotgun. Then there's the matter of the manure, melons, hay, and feed that frequently occupy the truck bed and the two dogs that run alongside the truck, stopping at every watering trough to cool off from

Jessica's dogs are trained to herd the cows. She will give them a command to move the cows in a certain direction, and if a cow breaks off from the herd, the dog will get the cow back with the rest of the herd.

the heat. It's not your ordinary office space, but it is a perfect fit for Jessica who deftly straddles her responsibilities as cattle rancher, watermelon farmer, and general contractor in Newberry, Florida, 20 miles west of Gainesville.

"I always wanted to be outside," Jessica says brightly about her diverse career choice. "My husband and I met in high school. Paul has always loved farming and raising cattle. He and his brother and dad own thirds in the family company—E.D. Norfleet & Sons, Inc., and Norfleet Cattle Co. We have 3,500 acres of pasture land, 1,500 head of momma cows, and 3,000 head of calves that we background." This is the term for when ranchers raise calves to a specific weight until they're ready to be shipped off to a feedlot or kept in the cattle market as commercial cows.

"A few years ago," Jessica continues, "Paul and I started our own construction company, P.W. Norfleet, LLC, where we just do roads and underground utilities. My father was always in construction. He's a general contractor. Even though I didn't come from a farming background, I always had horses. I was always interested in outside stuff. I slipped in the groove easy. It doesn't take long to learn something that you're passionate about."

Watermelon farming is her latest learning experience. "Newberry used to be the watermelon capital," Jessica teases. (Hope, Arkansas, and Cordele, Georgia, are currently battling for that title.) Her husband has fond memories of raising watermelon on his family's farm and decided he missed the drama. "He wanted to plant 50 acres of watermelon, so we did," she laughs. "But 98 percent of the farm is for cattle."

Do watermelon and cattle peaceably coexist? "Cattle *do love* watermelon!" Jessica giggles. "We keep watermelon in different fields from cows. Cows will get out if they

find a weak spot in the fence and will get into the watermelon. It's a heyday for them. Especially the younger cows. They'll run around like a kid in a candy store." A candy store filled with Jolly Rancher watermelon candies.

Jessica's two cattle dogs, Tater and Red, peaceably coexist with the cows as well. "The dogs are trained not to go after cows for no reason at all," Jessica tells me. She has a command that she uses if the dogs need to push the cows in a particular direction. "If a cow breaks out of the bunch, the dog will go get that particular cow. When the dog starts to get aggressive and bark, that's when the cows start to pay attention. Otherwise, the dogs really don't bother the cows. They each go on about their way."

Jessica and Paul have 50 acres devoted to watermelons.

In terms of a financial investment, Jessica explains that cattle are like raw material and there are natural cycles in every market. She's learning to prepare for and deal with those fluctuations. "It's a safe market because it's something that people need in good economic times or bad," she says. "But like with everything, when times are good you're saving up for when times are going to be bad. My husband's family has been in it for so long I can trust their instincts. When times are bad, they know it's happened before. They know we're gonna be all right."

Jessica knows her life looks different from most of her peers. It's hard to know if it's her age (25), gender, career choice, or a combination of these factors that makes her so unusual. "A lot of my friends are teachers or other professions and they think, 'Crazy Old Jessica,' because every time they call me up on my cell phone I'm on a horse. One or two of my friends are comfortable on a farm or around horses. The others are uncomfortable. Even the ones that are comfortable don't totally understand what I do on a day-to-day business."

It doesn't help that the day-to-day business looks different every day. As a cattle rancher, you might find Jessica working the cattle, moving them out to pasture, or bringing them into the cow pens and checking over the calves to make sure they have their proper shots. Attending to the pasture land might require planting new grasses, controlling the weeds, or mending a fence. When she's wearing her watermelon farmer hat, she might be checking for insect damage or replacing a part on the irrigation equipment. As a general contractor for infrastructure development, she's coordinating the efforts of various subcontractors, arranging for the delivery of pipe and fire hydrants, digging the sewer ditches, or contacting a supplier to check on a shipment of manholes.

"I wouldn't have it any other way," Jessica says. "We have cattle and construction. I work both. I enjoy dealing with people, but my heart is out at the farm. I prefer to be on the farm. I get satisfaction from seeing everything work out in nature. If you need rain, if you're patient, you'll finally get it. I love to be outside, being around all the animals. I don't feel unusual because it's what I enjoy and it's me. I feel comfortable with who I am."

She's definitely unusual for having a general contractor's license in Florida. "That is a big accomplishment here," she explains, "because the building codes are so strict. Most people say you have to take the licensing exam at least twice in order to pass. I met people at the test site who have been in the industry for 30 years, taking the test for their sixth and seventh time. I took it when I was 23 and I was probably one of four girls and 1,000 men taking the test. I was really worried when I saw that!" Jessica passed the test her first time taking it.

When asked if she feels her age or her gender has created any obstacles, Jessica readily admits, "That was a big issue for me. You always feel people are going to make

Tater and Red serve as Jessica's coworkers on the job.

you prove yourself more. That they're not going to think I know what I'm talking about. In some cases, I have to work harder to earn their respect, but I strive to work harder anyways from the beginning and they see that and appreciate that I'm doing it right. I have competitive prices. When I got my contractor's license, I envisioned it would be a long row to hoe but people have been very accepting. I'm doing what I say I'm going to do and they really appreciate that. Maybe because I was expecting it and preparing myself for it, but I didn't have a hard time."

Jessica brings other aspects of her personality to the job in addition to her infectious energy and friendliness. "I'm a terribly honest person," she tells me. "When I was in high school, whenever I did anything wrong, I always ended up telling the truth. I find that to be a real positive aspect in the way I do business and the way I am as a person. Sometimes it's hard to be the honest person because you're competing with dishonest people and you feel like maybe they have the advantage. But I feel so far I have been rewarded for being the honest person and doing what's right."

One of the biggest challenges facing the Florida cattle rancher today is the problem of encroaching development. Florida is one of the fastest-growing states in the union, according to fellow cattle rancher, Marcia Lightsey of Lightsey Cattle Company. Marcia, her husband, Cary, and his brother, Layne, own 30,000 acres of pastureland in the center of Florida, extending over three counties—Osceola, Polk, and Highlands. "Just 60 miles south of Mickey Mouse," Marcia jokes.

Jessica's pickup is constantly taking her all over the farm and surrounding area as she balances her life among the animals, watermelons, and the contracting business.

"Twelve hundred people are moving to Florida every day," she explains, "while at the same time, 500 acres of agricultural land is being converted to asphalt to put in a shopping center or mall or housing development. Farmers have got subdivisions right up on their fence line with people complaining that the cows smell. Florida has gotten so populated, ranchers are packing up, putting cattle on trailers, and moving to Texas."

There's also the problem with poachers. "People will come on your property and poach deer or cattle," Marcia tells me. "We've found bulls that have been shot and all they took was the hind quarter. People have shot a calf and drug it through the fence and loaded it into a car. We've found them in town later and they're skinning the calf in their garage. If they're caught taking livestock off your property, it's livestock theft. We've gone to court numerous times. It's not so bad nowadays because there's more activity around us. But it's still a big problem on the more isolated ranches."

Jessica has learned to handle not only the complications presented by each individual industry, but the areas where they intersect. "It's disheartening as a rancher and someone who loves land to see the land for sale everywhere. I'm part of this growth," she admits. "It makes it hard except for the fact that I develop parts that have already been developed and decided on. I'm not pushing zoning changes. I'm not putting together projects where people don't want them. I primarily work on the development in Gainesville and not out here in rural areas."

Although Jessica enjoys her work with the contracting business, her heart is always with the farm.

One of the biggest issues for Jessica has been the fluctuations in the raw materials market, such as concrete and steel. The cost of fuel prices in 2005 after Hurricane Katrina hit particularly hard. "It's a major issue in construction," she explains. "The rising cost of fuel, diesel, raw materials—it all affects our business. Asphalt is a petroleum-based product. You can't change your contract. You have a contract price. We've had to put clauses in the contract to protect ourselves."

Jessica is a study in motion and so are her shotguns. She shoots at coyotes, stray dogs, and buzzards to protect the calves. Coyotes and raccoons will also go after the watermelon. "I'll shoot buzzards," Jessica says without hesitation. "They'll eat the calves' eyes out. I'll shoot coyotes. That's my sport. My dogs run them down. Coyotes are not protected here. They're fair game." Keeping the cattle, calves, and watermelons safe, riding out the fluctuations in the cattle and construction market— are there any other challenges Jessica faces? "People try to hunt our deer. We don't hunt our deer. We just feed them and look at them." Frost on the watermelon is another challenge. "If it doesn't kill them, it will set them back and take longer for them to ripen," which in turn affects their market price. Then there are the labor issues. "There didn't used to be a problem with labor when it came time to pick, but recent immigration issues have changed all that. It's a problem for every farmer who is dependent on immigrant labor. It's not such a problem for us because our watermelons are not a mainstay—just a hobby. We just want to get our money back. But it's sad to see other farmers struggling. They had a good crop this year and couldn't get the labor to pick it."

Through it all, Jessica remains upbeat, optimistic, and true to her love of the land and her connection to animals. "Growing up," she says as she climbs back into her executive chair, "my dad told me, 'You can do anything your brother can do. If there's something you're passionate about, do it,' he said. 'Don't feel you have boundaries because you're a girl.'" Blowing right through those boundaries, Jessica drives her 4x4 office and her office mates, including a miniature dachshund named Oscar, to make a pitstop at the office coffee machine—a local coffee shop.

Jana Sweets

Tucson, Arizona

By Holly L. Bollinger

The hot and arid foothills of Arizona's Tucson Mountains is probably not the first place you'd expect someone who was raised in the cool, moist climate of Pennsylvania to settle down, but it is the only place Jana Sweets would consider calling home.

"I love it out here," Jana says emphatically, "You either love it or you hate it."

Jana is the founder and co-owner of Sticky Situation, her 20-year-old desert plant farm and nursery located just outside Tucson. Jana and Kim Joyiens, her business partner for nearly a decade, produce thousands of cacti and other succulents in hundreds of varieties from around the world. The team grows its plants from seeds and cuttings in four greenhouses and two acres of ground beds.

Jana got herself into her present-day Sticky Situation by making her childhood dream come true. Jana's mom was raised on a farm in Arizona where Jana's grandparents had first homesteaded during the Great Depression in the late 1920s and early 1930s. After her mother had married her father, Jana's mom agreed to move to Pennsylvania to live and raise their family amidst the civilized society of the East. "Temporary insanity, you know," says Jana with a laugh.

It was in Jana's home state, where tree-laden forests of state parks can be found every 25 miles in any direction from any given point on the Pennsylvania map, that she first learned to appreciate all things green. As a child, she enjoyed planting and

For the past 20 years, Jana Sweets has owned and operated Sticky Situation desert plant farm and nursery.

OPPOSITE PAGE:
This is one of Jana's pets that roam around Sticky Situation.

80

Sticky Situation has four greenhouses and two acres of ground beds.

tending a section of her parents' yard where her mother encouraged Jana to grow a garden to her own liking. Later, Jana's mom introduced her to a Pennsylvania farmer who grew cacti up to the ceiling of his greenhouse. Right away Jana took to the prickly plants and saw them as a wonderment of nature.

As Jana continued to grow into adolescence, she took with her the penchant for plants, including cacti. When it was time to consider her college education, Jana knew what she wanted to pursue—a degree in horticulture. That's when her parents realized that their daughter's childhood hobby was becoming her lifelong passion.

Looking back, Jana says her parents never hesitated to support her dreams. She remembers their encouragement, "If I could go to college and go to do what I liked, then that was all the better. They never tried to push me to be a doctor or a lawyer, and I'm grateful for that."

Jana and her parents moved west in the late 1970s, and she earned her Bachelor of Science degree in agriculture, majoring in horticulture, from the University of Arizona in 1982. She worked in local nurseries throughout college and learned even more about raising cacti and other succulents.

Around the time she was ready to embark on a career, Jana's parents bought two four-acre lots in a spacious neighborhood several miles above the bustle of downtown Tucson. After gaining a few more years of work experience, Jana was ready to set the stakes for her dream oasis in the desert and fill it with cacti and other water-conserving plants. In 1990, she began building Sticky Situation's final home next door to her parents in the open-air desert that Jana and her mom love so much.

Thousands of cacti and succulents from hundreds of worldwide varieties are grown at the farm nestled at the base of the Tucson Mountains in Arizona.

When Jana first started her own commercial business, she used her green-thumb skills to grow herbs as well as cacti. After only a few seasons, she discovered that cultivating herbs, even within the safety of a greenhouse, consumed too much time and resources for the return. "If it wasn't the whiteflies, it was a fungus," she recalls about the effort. "There was always a need for an insecticide or herbicide treatment."

Another one of Jana's early endeavors involved supplying retail stock for one of Tucson's Kmart stores in the early 1990s. That particular store had a large lawn and garden center, and Jana was the exclusive supplier for its herbs and desert plants. "That was a really good deal at the time," she says. "I had the prime spot in the best-selling part of one of the biggest Kmart garden sections in the Southwest, and all I had to do was keep it full all the time. I thought, 'This is great!' Until I had to keep going in there, and I'd see how people would dump the pots on the floor and the plants would just lay there for a week."

The customers' lack of respect for the plants and the store's carelessness in taking care of the garden section turned Jana off from the commercial agreement that brought her thousands of dollars in annual revenue. "I decided it was time to ask for a divorce. I just said, 'I don't need you.' And even though I took a big pay cut, it was worth it to get away from that."

Jana says she was hurt by the way the corporate entity and the people shopping took her efforts for granted. But ultimately, it was the blatant disregard for the life of the tiny plants that helped her to make up her mind. "I knew it would have eventually driven me insane to keep seeing that. Maybe a lot of people thought I was being too sensitive, but how could you not be when you care so much about your work?"

Today Jana grows more than 300 varieties of plants that are native to desert climates from every corner of the globe. From exotic to simple—she says Central and South America offer some of the world's most beautiful flowering cacti and Africa produces the lushest varieties of succulents—Jana grows them all. Euphorbias and some of the other semitropical succulents boast leaves of a sort that don't really look like cacti at all. "Some of them look like they're from another world," Jana says.

It takes about two years for a cactus to grow from a seed to 2 inches high. Jana carefully waters and tends to her plants and thinks of them as her children.

Of the more popular species, she grows certain ones into the thousands so that the nursery always has enough of the better-selling varieties on hand for customer demand. It's not really a concern if a cactus isn't sold in its 3-inch-pot stage one season, says Jana, because it can grow up to a 5-inch pot just in time for the next year's sales.

The care and nurturing of growing even a single cactus requires more time and patience than is apparent to most people when they see the spiny, fleshy mound. Though it is essentially drought-resistant, a cactus needs the right amount of water and nutrients to survive.

Over the years, Jana has become very attached to her nursery stock. She says the plants have become much like children to her, especially because she's invested so much time, money, and effort in rearing them. A typical cactus takes about 2 years to grow from seed to a very small 2 inches in height. Yet Jana has raised some cacti in the rocky, sand-packed soils of her ground beds for as many as 18 years. She points out that a similar cactus in the wild would take 40 or 50 years to grow to the same 3- and 4-foot stature as her nursery-tended giants.

Even more than the satisfaction she gets from seeing her cacti flourish, Jana is proud of the water conservation her nursery promotes. Her monthly water bill during the summer months is less for the greenhouses and outdoor plots than for the house.

Conserving water is essential to living in the desert. According to Jana, there are two rainy seasons in her part of the Sonoran Desert, which stretches over 120,000 square miles from southwestern Arizona and southeastern California through most of Baja California and to the western half of Mexico's state of Sonora.

Jana's love of cacti goes back to her childhood in Pennsylvania when her parents introduced her to a local grower whose cacti reached the ceiling of his greenhouse.

The winter rains fall during January and February, and the summer rainy season lasts from about July through September. But the calendar doesn't guarantee rainfall. "Some years it rains a lot and other years we go nine months without rain."

Even during extended periods of drought, the Sticky Situation cacti survive and thrive under Jana's watchful eye. In the searing heat of 100-plus degrees, Jana thoroughly waters the plants once a week. But in the winter months, she waters on an extended monthly basis and not at all when there's a potential for freezing nighttime temperatures.

Yet, it's during the driest, hottest months that a cactus faces the most danger—not from lack of water, but from the attention of predators. "The bigger (the plants') spines, the better," Jana says. "If they just have some little, wimpy spines, they become food and all that's left is a pile of stickers." Of all the desert animals that

Water conservation is always important, but especially during the blistering summer heat. Jana prides herself on her low water bills during the dry months.

wander into the neighborhood, sometimes the smallest creatures pose the biggest threat to Jana's stock.

Desert packrats, which look more like big gerbils than the common image rats may conjure up, can eat up to $1,000 in plants in one night. Lately the nursery has had to resort to using traps for the rodents. Jana says that she hates to do it, but feels she has no choice. For years, she tried keeping pet cats on her property, but the approach proved too disheartening over time when larger prey, like owls and coyotes, continually nabbed her feline guards.

Overall, Jana likes the quiet wild of the habitat surrounding her. But as Tucson continues to grow up around the foothills, more and more people are moving into the desert suburbs. Jana has a 360-degree view of the city's urban sprawl, and her desert sanctuary is not as full of wildlife as it once was. However, she knows it's the people who live in the urban and suburban areas that make up the majority of her customers. She tries to get to know her customers and invite them to call for appointments so she can provide the best one-on-one service in person.

Jana has the science of consumer marketing down pat. "You have certain times of [the] year when you're heavy into selling, and the certain times of year when you're heavy into planting." Mid- to late summer is Jana's heaviest planting season, and she sells more in the fall, winter, and spring.

One of her favorite ways to show off her cactus varieties is during local and regional arts and crafts fairs. Fairs draw in a lot of people and give Jana an opportunity not only to sell her plants, but also to educate her customers in person about the care and nurturing of their new family additions.

In Jana's experience, most people are unfamiliar with succulents and seem to misunderstand the beauty of any cactus. "Kids, of course, will want to touch them," Jana muses. She says that more often than not, parents pull their children back and warn them, "'Don't touch that; it's dangerous.' Kids aren't stupid, you know. It only takes once. They're just as smart as animals, and once an animal gets poked in the nose, it doesn't usually come back a second time." She adds, "I'm sure glad my mom didn't raise me to be afraid, or I wouldn't be doing this today."

Pricked fingers are an occupational hazard for Jana. Wrapping her fingers in tape allows her to touch the cacti with less pain.

Ultimately, Jana knows that it's her love of the cactus that allows her to appreciate, more than most, the many varieties of desert succulents she raises. She believes that if others better understood the way a cactus works, then they could just as wholeheartedly come to appreciate them. "The ugliest cactus blooms the most beautiful flowers," she says. "I think it's Mother Nature's way of showing us there's purpose in everything."

Nancy Wilson

Fossil, Oregon

By Bethany Weaver-Culpepper and Susan Gartner

Nancy Wilson grew up on a ranch and wouldn't think of living any other way.

OPPOSITE PAGE:
Nancy and her husband, Phil, operate a cattle ranch and bed and breakfast on land that has been in Phil's family since the late 1800s.

NEXT PAGE:
Nancy and Phil's guests participate in cattle drives on the property near the Cascade Mountains in Oregon.

Standing at the highest point of the property at sunset overlooking the Cascade Mountains is an assault on your senses. Taking in the smell of the sage and juniper is like taking an aroma bath. You feel embraced by the universe and like you're the luckiest person alive. Wilson Ranches Retreat has a way of making people feel this way. Nancy Wilson and her husband, Phil, own and operate the 9,000-acre working cattle ranch and bed and breakfast in Fossil, Oregon.

"There's not a stranger that walks through that door," says Nancy and Phil's youngest daughter, Kara. "No one leaves without a hug. When you're with my mom and dad, you're family."

Fossil, population 450, is located 180 miles southeast of Portland, Oregon. "There's only three ways out of Fossil," jokes Phil. One is through high desert, one is through high timber, and one is through high plateau wheat fields. In order to make sure their guests experience the full spectrum of what the area has to offer, if guests come in through the wheat fields—"We send them the other two ways!" laughs Nancy. One of the retreat's secret pleasures is the sunset tour. Folks don't always know to inquire about it, unless someone happens to mention it at breakfast. "Up on the mountains there are no cars, no sirens, no lights," says Nancy. "It's God's universe."

Nancy and Phil live in the area Phil's family homesteaded in the late 1800s. They have three children—two daughters and a son. Milne and her family have chosen a

similar life in agriculture in central Oregon. Kara and her family live in Houston, Texas. Zane lives and works on the family ranch with his folks. There are four grandchildren, ages 6 months to 13 years, who all ride horses and help move cattle with Nancy and Phil. Nancy wants to be remembered as "an awesome grandmother, loving and kind." Her eight-year-old grandson asked her, "Babushka ['Grandma' in Russian], are you going to be alive when I'm an adult?" She replied that she hopes so. He then stated, "You'll be my best friend."

Raised on a ranch in Kimberly, Oregon, with four older sisters and one younger brother, Nancy and her father would have never gotten off their horses if Nancy's mother hadn't intervened and taught her the tasks of cooking, sewing, gardening, and taking care of people. "What came first was to be a rancher's wife," Nancy remembers.

"So much of the woman my mom is now is through the experience of growing up on a ranch," Kara proudly says of her mother. "Anything my grandpa required from a hired hand, he required from his daughters. They had a rough life. They were hardworking kids, hardworking young women. That was ingrained in her. She has a tremendous care of their cattle. It's beautiful how much she loves their life."

"I didn't know we were poor growing up," Nancy admits. "I thought we were wealthy." She and her family took care of the horses and cows, and they always had hired help eating at their table. Her mother made clothes for her family. Nancy always had enough and felt like she lived in a castle.

"Her home was a castle because that's how you felt," Kara confirms. "My mom grew up in a home so full of love you didn't know you didn't have the best of things."

Nancy's first horse was given to her by her dad when she was four years old. Sparky gave her one colt per year, which she was responsible for training. She wore a path around their house running her horse at breakneck speed. "On my horse," says Nancy, "I'm a kid at heart." Horse racing was a part of her life. "With any horse, you have certain rules. You treat them good because he's number one in your life. He needs his grain as much as you or even more." Unfortunately for the horse, there is competition for that number one spot in Nancy's life—her husband, Phil. "I met the love of my life in eighth grade," says Nancy with a smile.

The local 4-H Club has a summer school for eighth grade through high school that takes place at Oregon State University. "Kids from all counties go and stay in dorm rooms," explains Nancy. "You're right on campus, just like the college kids. It's a pretty big deal." It was there that she met Phil. "I came home from summer school and told my mama and sister I met the guy I'm gonna marry. They thought it was the funniest thing they'd ever heard."

Nancy and Phil didn't see each other again until the summer of their junior year of high school. "He said he was going to write me, but he lost his crayons," Nancy jokes. They met again at the same 4-H summer school and started to date. Phil had told his dad that he wanted to live on the family ranch after he graduated from college. "He was a steward of the land, even then," Nancy recalls. "A rancher at heart. That's how I knew he was the one. I knew. My mama knew." They got married when they were 19 and 20 years old.

Two years ago, Nancy and Phil were entertaining guests and sitting on their hill watching the sunset over Mt. Hood when their visitors asked them how they met. Phil told them, "We became soul mates in the eighth grade." Nancy's eyes almost popped out of her head. "We've been married 34 years," she told her guests, "and he's never told me this."

In addition to managing 400 head of beef cows, there are also the 950 tons of hay to grow and put up to feed the cattle. A major concern has been the amount of rainfall. Fossil averages approximately 10 to 16 inches of rain per year. Although there has been a drought for the past 10 years, two ponds that had been dry for 12 years

Nancy and Phil keep an eye on their 9,000 acres on horseback.

finally have water again. Nancy says they have the only green hay fields in the area because of a creek that helps irrigate the land. Fresh spring water feeds three of the four houses on the ranch.

Drought is an issue, but there's a much bigger problem facing cattle ranchers today. "Only one percent of the U.S. population is involved in family farms and ranches," Nancy points out. "And that figure is getting smaller." Big corporations are coming in and buying the family farms and cattle ranches. They plan to either use the land as a tax write-off, or to split it up and sell smaller sections to subdivide for homes. "People can't work these smaller sections as a cattle ranch. They're taking away the American ranch," Nancy sadly says.

"Some of our richest soil for farming and most beautiful land for grazing livestock is being taken and covered with cement for shopping malls," says Kara. "It's being turned into buildings and parking lots, and you can't get it back. That's the heartache for farmers and ranchers—to see our beautiful land ripped and a building or home goes up in its place and it never goes back to its God-given beauty."

In 1997, the bank told Nancy and Phil that they were not going to make it financially and they should sell. They dug in their heels and resolved to find a way to keep the ranch because "once it's gone," Nancy says, "you can't get it back."

The web site for the Wilson Ranches Retreat Bed and Breakfast claims it's "The Best Rest in Wheeler County. Joy for the Heart, Peace for the Soul, and Memories for a Lifetime." The idea for a B&B wasn't so outrageous. Nancy and Phil had so many people visiting their ranch that it seemed like a logical step. Their first official guests

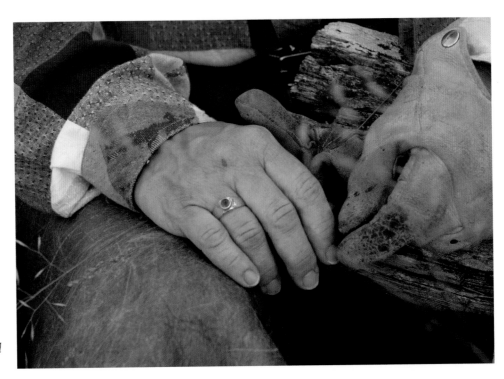

These strong hands have seen plenty of hard work, but have loved and nurtured three children and four grandchildren.

arrived on March 12, 2000. Six years later, they have hit the 10,000th guest mark and are thrilled with the high rate of return. Through the past six years, they have seen young children grow as they return with their families. "The biggest blessing is that we're bringing the world to us," Nancy says. "We're meeting people from all over the world."

One of their guests was a man on a motorcycle who drove up on a busy Memorial Day weekend and wanted to know if they had any rooms available. Fortunately, they did. After some time, Nancy went up to the room to make sure everything was okay. The man turned to her in tears. She hugged him, not quite knowing what to make of it. His wife had died a year earlier, he told her, and he took this trip as a way to heal, not knowing the destination. When he walked into the room, he was greeted with the same bedspread that he and his wife had shared.

Nancy has a special gift for making people feel at home. That's what keeps people coming back—that and the full country breakfast they serve every morning. Phil is the main cook and cowboy storyteller. "It was his idea to have the B&B," Nancy says playfully, "so he has to cook." Guests mingle in the kitchen and dining room in anticipation of the country-fried steak, scrambled eggs, and homemade biscuits prepared by Phil and Nancy. Fifteen to 20 guests can comfortably be seated around the table while Phil entertains them with stories of the ranch.

A favorite story is about Phil getting bit by a rattlesnake as he was cutting hay. He didn't think twice about it and went about his chores, all the while his hand was swelling up. They finally decided to call a doctor who told them to immediately go to the nearest hospital. A ride into town was a rare treat, so when they got near the hospital five hours later, Nancy used the opportunity to run into a jewelry store to get a battery for her watch, which Phil didn't mind in the least. When Nancy returned, Phil was nowhere in sight. Nancy started to panic—Where did he go? Was he all right? A few minutes later when Phil showed up, she asked, "Where did you go?" He replied, "You went to get a battery, I went to get gum." (Phil survived both the snake and the shopping attack.)

The table is set for the guests of Wilson Ranches Retreat where the guests are treated like family.

The idea of opening the bed and breakfast was conceived as a quick fix to save the farm. After six years of operation, the Wilsons have had over 10,000 guests stay at their B&B.

There are many activities to partake in at the retreat: horseback riding, cattle drives, hiking, mountain biking, fishing, photography, or just being quiet enough to observe the local wildlife.

"Today we had 15 for breakfast," Nancy relates. "Afterward, I cleaned and put things away. I have one person a day that helps me clean. Then we saddled the horses and took five people on a horseback ride for an hour. Another group is coming in 10 minutes and they'll be riding for five hours, moving cattle." *Moving cattle?* "Clever, eh?" Nancy says with a grin. "We use them to help get our work done!" In reality, guests are free to choose what they want to do. "If they don't want to go, they don't have to," she confesses. "But they never would get a chance to do something like that. That's part of the fun!"

Unfortunately, experiences like this will only become more rare. "Our ranch is fifth generation," Kara explains. "I am sixth generation. There are very few fifth-generation men and women who want a life in agriculture because it is a hard life and not a life you get rich in. You're rich in the sense of simplicity and beauty and passion for the work, but not in money. In agriculture, each generation is building a life for the next generation. That's different than so many other careers. A lot of these families are having to sell because it's hard to get people to work for them; people that have that hard work ethic and passion for it. Farmers and ranchers and dairies have really been hit hard in the northwest. We have friends who are now buying into a dairy that's not even in their family because there's no one to take it on. The pioneers that exist now, my dad's parents and my mom and dad—they're still in that life. They're still working so hard to keep it and make it better and inviting others to experience that and cherish it."

Kara laughs when she talks about how much guests enjoy spending time with her parents learning about their ranching life. "You could get up in the morning, have breakfast with Mom and Dad, and not leave the table until it's time for bed!"

"Every day," Kara continues, "people walk through their door and have no idea of the adversity and challenges facing the cattlemen today. They don't know when they vote on something how it's going to affect Mom and Dad's life—the most beautiful stewards of the land. Who are the true environmentalists? The men and women who depend on the land for their livelihood. There are so many people in our urban areas who are making decisions about the land, yet they have no idea of how it's affecting the land. With the bed and breakfast, my parents have a beautiful way to educate people. This is the kind of life we want to protect."

Kara's obvious respect for the land and life of a rancher was instilled in her at a very young age. "When the kids were 6 months old," Nancy relayed, "we started taking them with us to work the cattle. While cattle were grazing at a water hole, we'd get off the horses and have lunch. That's the part about a family ranch—the kids are part of your life when you're branding, on the tractor, moving cattle. You don't leave them with the babysitter."

"The people who come here are experiencing a history that they will rarely get a chance to experience in today's world," Kara says passionately. "They can come and share a story with their grandchildren about cowboys and cowgirls and the pioneers coming to Oregon and starting these farms and ranches. Hands-on experience about a life that still exists today. How many kids get to touch what's actually in the history books?"

The love of the land and tradition is something that Nancy has passed down to her daughter Kara.

Carolyn Lattin

Olympia, Washington

By Holly L. Bollinger

Debbie and Carolyn Lattin and Sherrie Kohlmann are the women behind the Lattin's Country Cider Mill and Farm in Olympia, Washington.

Opposite Page:
Locally grown products are an important and integral part of the farm's store.

Sure, it's been said that all work and no play makes Jack a dull boy. But it turns out that a life of hard work and doing something you love makes for some really good cider.

"We kind of work a little late every night," says Carolyn Lattin, about a typical evening, which can go well into the 9 o'clock hour at the Lattin's Country Cider Mill and Farm in Olympia, Washington. "Some days are really long and other days aren't." Those short days Carolyn is refering to only last about 11 hours on average, she says.

But Carolyn and her daughters, Debbie and Sherrie, say they wouldn't change a thing. "We just love what we do. It's a fun thing. It isn't like going to a job; it's just kind of a way of life. We work up here long, long hours, but you can't count out all of the hours because half of them are fun," Carolyn adds. "So it's not hard to put in all the hours. Now, if I worked for someone else, it would be totally different."

Carolyn owns and operates her 32-acre farm and small commercial cider mill in a part of Washington known for its waterways, volcanoes, and scenic national parks, but not for its apple growing. "We're kind of diversified here," says Carolyn. "We do a farm and we raise tremendous vegetables and pumpkins and corn—in fact, we don't raise a lot of fruit because this is western Washington and we just don't have the hot enough climate for it."

Every apple that goes into the cider press is inspected. If there are any bruises or spots on the apple, the offending part is cut off to ensure the quality of the apple cider is the best it can be.

Carolyn can grow soft summer apples, but not the longer-season varieties, such as Granny Smith or Red Delicious. At one point in her cider mill's 31-year history, Carolyn says she tried to harvest the 36 short-season apple trees, but soon discovered good labor was hard to find. "There's a trick to every trade. And if that's your job to pick strawberries or apples or whatever, you can do it real speedily. Whereas somebody who's never done it before, they're just a lot slower," she says, "Most people around here have never picked an apple from an apple tree."

The mill trucks in its apples—anywhere from 25,000 to 75,000 pounds, up to two semi loads, a week—from growers farther east where more than 225,000 acres of orchards thrive in the foothills of the Cascade Mountains. "But we're small," Carolyn insists.

Berries grow abundantly in the region, says Carolyn. Although she doesn't grow berries on her farm, she annually buys about $20,000 worth of different local berries, including blueberries, blackberries, strawberries, and raspberries. She uses the berries in fresh pies, jams, and syrups, but the majority of the tiny fruit is pulverized and used to naturally flavor their famously sweet apple ciders. "It's just 100 percent fruit juice," says Carolyn. "So when you drink it, it's going to taste just like eating an apple, but you don't have to chew."

Sounds good? Carolyn laughs as she proudly says, "Well, we've won six national awards." Their most recent include two first-place finishes in the same year, at the Illinois State Horticulture Society Specialty Crops Conference in the Midwest and the North American Direct Farm Marketing Show in Sacramento, California.

Despite the huge popularity of Lattin's cider, Carolyn's distribution chain is fundamentally tied to the local region. She says it costs about double the price for a gallon of the cider to ship anywhere else because of its weight and refrigeration needs. "We go as far as we can and get back within 12 hours," she says. The route through western Washington can go as far as 150 miles one way south to Woodland, Washington, near the Oregon border. The cider travels another 100 miles on the route to the east.

Carolyn says they continue to deliver their own product using refrigerated trucks so they know it's getting to the stores in the right condition. "We produce the cider for order," she says, "so we make the cider one day, and it gets in the stores by the next morning. And then it has a three-week shelf life.

"Now you'd be hard-pressed to squeeze orange juice and have it keep three weeks," says Carolyn. "The reason ours keeps so well is every single apple that's made into cider, we look it over and if there's any kind of break in the skin we cut that out." Leaving little-to-no bacteria in the fruit flesh to subsequently multiply in the pulverized apples, combined with the pasteurization process of heating the cider to 160 degrees Fahrenheit for 15 seconds, keeps the cider's freshly pressed taste from deteriorating.

"We're just real fussy with our product," Carolyn reiterates. "Your product is only as good as the raw material going in. We have five people who stand at the machine to be sure there is nothing that's going to get into our cider that would add any kind of bacteria into it. There's a lot of wild yeast on the outside of the fruit, but those apples

are absolutely perfect when they go in that grinder." She says the process is painstaking and that her crew does a lot of cutting on the apples, taking out bruises and stubborn or broken stems.

Carolyn says she's seen truckloads of apples that had been sitting in the sun, including rotten apples, that were swarming with fruit flies and fermentation running out the truck's bottom go into the mashers and boilers at big juice companies. Unbelievably, she says that it doesn't taste moldy. The difference is that cider is fresh, but apple juice goes through a whole commercial juice-making process, which includes boiling, straining, and stringent filtration. Cider and apple juice just don't compare, she says.

Although, according to Carolyn, there was once an organic cider company in Olympia that competed with Lattin's for a time but it was eventually shut down by the health department. "It was a wonderful thing when they went out of business because they gave cider a bad name," she says. "But they gave us a lot of problems because they were trying to make an inferior product and sell it as organic. We lost some of our accounts because of that. But you know, what goes around, comes around." Carolyn's market reach today is proof enough.

Lattin's supplies fresh cider to Food Services of America (a Pacific Northwestern food distribution company that delivers the cider to restaurants, schools, and hospitals), supermarkets, four juice companies, as well as many restaurants and local landmarks, such as the Space Needle in Seattle, Timberline Lodge on Mt. Hood, and shops in Seaside, Oregon.

The days can be long at the Lattins' farm, but thanks to the wonderful crew, the hours are so full of fun and laughter that it's not hard to put in long hours.

Carolyn drizzles frosting over her famous apple fritters. She sells an average of 27,000 apple fritters a year.

"That's what really carries us with the rest of it [the farm]. But we are tremendously busy with the farming bit of it from the first of April until the first of October," says Carolyn. "Our cider carries us because there's not a lot of money in growing vegetables." She adds, "We're hiring kids who have never seen a carrot grow, so they don't know the difference between a carrot and a weed. And they don't want to do that kind of work. They want to sit in front of the computer." Carolyn says they tend not to hire teens and 20-somethings because of their lack of hands-on skills when it comes to gardening and farming. "There's nobody that is raised to do that kind of work anymore."

Carolyn says she's happy with her middle-aged workforce, which is made up of 15 locals. "A lot of the time they've had their own gardens. And they know how to show up for work and dress appropriately."

The farm keeps going and Carolyn's customer base continues to grow—now well into its third generation of the same families that started buying produce from her 50 years ago. But the city of Olympia may be outgrowing her farm.

"We're about three and a half miles outside of Olympia," says Carolyn, quickly adding, "Unfortunately. I wish we were 20 miles farther because the price of land is going up so rapidly that it's going to be hard for us to justify raising pumpkins."

But with her $1 million-plus investment in cold rooms, freezers, cider press equipment, and an in-house bakery, Carolyn says she will never consider moving. She's content to see that the business is constantly evolving. Her business plan has always been to use most of the revenue for improving the farm and mill equipment, including the truck fleet, and for the throngs of ongoing public relations efforts.

Carolyn describes the farm as divided into thirds: one-third vegetables and pumpkins, one-third animal pasture (also used for occasional parking), and one-third is wooded, which doubles as an animal housing area during the many events they host throughout the year.

The calendar of events at Lattin's is extensive. They hid more than 36,000 Easter eggs for the annual hunt in spring 2006. One weekend in September is always slotted for their Apple Festival, when they sell up to 1,400 apple fritters in one day. Then, there's October's much anticipated month-long pumpkin season, during which they provide free wagon rides, a petting zoo, and haunted houses as additional entertainment for visitors.

A typical fair-type weekend brings an average of 500 cars, carrying around 1,000 people, to the farm. To avoid disgruntled car owners who were getting trapped by her other customers' poor self-parking attempts, Carolyn recently had to hire parking attendants. The added expense forced her to charge a meager $2 per car for parking. "Some people still object to the $2 parking." But they certainly don't mind the free wagon rides, she adds, which costs Lattin's several hundred dollars in horse rental and feed alone.

Never mind the handful of naysayers, Lattin's Country Cider Mill and Farm is a consistent favorite for family outings in the community. "Our local paper loves us. They know how much we give back to the community. They try to support us very much; they have written a lot of articles on us. A lot of them come out here and shop, who do the writing, too, so they know us personally," she says.

Having a clean place is important to Carolyn. Keeping the animals tidy and taking care of the landscaping are among her priorities, all of which have attributed to Lattin's good reputation among customers. "We don't use any pesticides because we don't need to," says Carolyn. "If we were growing commercial broccoli where you have fields and fields, then the bugs would get started. We don't say 'organic,' we just say, 'no pesticides.'"

Years ago, Carolyn was one of four founders of the Olympia farmers' market. Lattin's Farm operated a stand at the market five days a week for 17 years. But the farm demanded more time than she could afford to spend at the market, so today Carolyn enjoys the success of selling the produce directly from the farm; processed and baked products are popular sellers, including 24 types of jams and 24 varieties of pies; and the apple fritters, of which she sells more than 27,000 every year.

Lattin's Country Cider Mill buys locally grown berries to make its homemade syrup.

"Nobody does what we do in our area. There's one fellow down the road who grows sweet corn and he uses our cold room for storage. But there's not a lot [of] farming because people just don't want to work that hard anymore," she says.

Carolyn doesn't hesitate to say that farming is hard work because she's experienced it first-hand every minute in building her farm from the ground up.

"We've been on this farm for 50 years and we started out as a chicken venture," she says about her and her husband, Vic's, humble beginning. "We built a building and we had one flock of chickens with 1,500 chickens. We sold eggs for 19 cents a dozen. They were in a carton, candled and weighed, and washed. And we lost our shirt. We owed $7,000 at the end of those two years. That doesn't sound like much, except that in 1955, $7,000 was more like $70,000 today." The couple was forced to sell the chickens, but they kept the outbuilding for storing hay.

One nondescript day thereafter, they bought a hand-cider press and began making cider for themselves and their neighbors. It was so delicious that their neighbors, who were planning to open a restaurant, requested to put the Lattins' cider on their menu. At the time, Carolyn and Vic declined because of all the formalities involved in getting licensed to sell their cider commercially. But a year later, their legendary cider business was born. "January the 20th of the next year, they called us and said that they had the restaurant going and they wanted 10 gallons of cider."

The Lattins decided the time was right to try their hand at a new venture so they called around, to no avail at first, looking for a grower willing to part with the scant amount of apples they needed. "Most of the time, they hung up on us when they found out that we wanted a bin of apples," says Carolyn, "because most of them were under contract with the co-op to buy all of their apples."

During the fall, the farm has pumpkins for sale and hosts many activities, such as a petting zoo and haunted house.

They did find a grower and turned 900 pounds of apples into their first order for cider. That one delivery catapulted them into the cider-making business. "Well, this one told that one, and that one told another," says Carolyn about the word-of-mouth spread of rave reviews. They quickly moved into using all stainless-steel equipment, including a new cider press, for which they had to travel all the way to Goshen, Indiana, to purchase.

After awhile, Carolyn tried to branch out into the mainstream community with her cider. But she soon discovered that most people weren't even aware of sweet cider. "You know how many teenage kids are going to try a glass of cider when they have a Coke in their hands? Not very many."

That's when Carolyn took marketing efforts into her own hands. "When I realized down at a fair that no one wanted to try the cider, I came home, I got the phone book out. I called every daycare in the phone book and said, 'Come out for free. You can make your own cider and taste it.' And so they all came out. I did it for free for quite a few years until I realized that every child that came through here was costing me 50 cents at that time. I was sending them home with a little half-pint of cider, and it took thousands of dollars to PR the product.

"Even today, there are children who come out on a cider tour and have never, ever tasted freshly pressed apple cider. And so it's taken a lot of PR to get people to try it. Sometimes when I offer it to somebody, they say, 'Well, we don't like cider.' And then when they taste it, they say, 'Well, this is really good.'" Carolyn agrees; "Yeah, it is."

Carolyn has a way about her, whether it's persuading people to try cider or using her ability to make ends meet. "I am 74, and I was born ambitious," she says. "When we got this farm, it cost $15,000 to buy a 32-acre farm with a brand new house and a barn and a tractor. Our payments were $115 a month and my husband's take-home pay was $115. We postponed our family for 10 years because we had to make the payments on the farm. I froze everything that I could possibly freeze because my salary went to pay for a car payment, our gas, our food, our payment on a second-hand refrigerator and a second-hand oil stove and a sewing machine. There just wasn't a lot left."

Vic was born and raised in Seattle. He studied and worked at the University of Washington. Carolyn grew up in eastern Washington on a wheat ranch. Later she went to work in Olympia as a secretary for her cousin, who was a senator. Carolyn remembers that one day the chief accountant for the office went to the university looking to hire someone with an accounting degree who would be willing to learn computer skills. Vic Lattin came to her office for an interview and Carolyn was smitten. "I told the chief accountant, 'If you hire him, I'll marry him.' And I did."

When her husband died a few years ago, the family lost their treasured accountant, in addition to their cherished loved one. "It's like one leg gone from the table. We miss his presence in many ways," Carolyn says. "He made us all promise to keep it [the farm] going."

Their two daughters have stayed in the business and will take over for Carolyn one day. "My two sons escaped and they've got real jobs," she adds teasingly. "And the girls—I make them feel guilty so they don't leave me."

Her oldest daughter, Debbie, lives on the farm full-time with her mom. "This is just wonderful for her and me both," says Carolyn, "We really enjoy each other's company. The girls feel the same way about the business as I do, and so I don't think they're going anywhere fast. They really enjoy what they do. They're doing it because of that, and it isn't hard to put in a lot of time."

As the oldest in nine children, Carolyn had to learn how to farm with horses and cook for the farmhands before her family could afford their first tractor (bought when she was in high school). She learned the value of a strong work ethic early in life. "I learned to work, and my children have learned to work.

"My oldest son said once, 'You know, Mom, I'm never going to do like you and Dad, work seven days a week.' He said, 'I'm working for the state and I'm going to take my weekends off. And I'm going to enjoy life. I'm not just going to work all the time.'

"One night, a Sunday night, it was about 9 o'clock, he said, 'I've got to leave. I better go back to work.'" Carolyn says she was amused. "'Well, what happened?' I asked. 'You were going to have your weekends off.' He said, 'Mom, you've got to put in some extra time or you'll never get anyplace.'"

As she retells the story, Carolyn laughs and ends the story with a definitive statement. "An apple doesn't fall far from the tree."

The Country Cider Mill makes 24 varieties of pies and 24 different jams from locally grown berries.

Julie Safley
Hillsboro, Oregon

By Holly L. Bollinger

Julie Safley, along with her husband, Michael, own and operate the Northwest Alpacas Ranch near Hillsboro, Oregon.

OPPOSITE PAGE:
Alpacas were first imported to the United States from South America in 1984. Julie's husband was one of the four original alpaca farmers.

You can buy just about anything on the Internet these days, even alpacas. As unique Internet sales pitches go, the slogan on Julie Safley's Northwest Alpacas home page is pretty hard to beat: "Alpaca shopping from the comfort of your home. We ship anywhere in the United States."

Julie and her husband, Michael, own and operate the Northwest Alpacas Ranch in Hillsboro, Oregon. They also operate one of the industry's most prominent web sites, www.alpacas.com, which offers a searchable online sales catalog of more than 200 individual animals, complete with each one's registered name, an up-to-date photo, genetic profile, microchip number, and fiber details. Prices for their stock range from around $1,000 to well over $20,000.

Most of the animals for sale online are of the Huacaya breed (pronounced wah-KI-ya), which produce a fluffy fiber suited for knitting, crocheting, and weaving, according to Julie. The other breed of alpacas is the Suri, recognizable for its long and silky dreadlock-type hair, which is best for weaving. "Certain weaving techniques will result in a Suri coat resembling a fur pelt coat; pure elegance," Julie says.

Alpacas, which are native to South America, are temperate animals that resemble llamas on a smaller, more compact scale. "You compare a llama to an alpaca," says Julie, "and it's [alpaca] half the size. It's much gentler. It's easier to handle as a livestock animal."

Baby alpacas are called crias. Once the female crias are 18 months old, they can be bred.

Most alpacas grow to a height of just more than 3 feet at the withers and a weight of around 150 pounds at adulthood. The alpaca is notably docile for its size. "They're just so easy to raise," says Julie. "They have padded feet so they don't damage the pasture grass." Once in awhile a stud male might get a bit aggressive, but Julie comments that's just in its nature during breeding season.

Unlike the ambiguous beginnings of many types of today's domestic livestock in the United States, the more recent introduction of alpaca herds stateside makes their American lineage much easier to pinpoint. Michael Safley was among the first group of Americans to buy 5 of the 50 alpacas that were initially imported from South America in 1984. Julie's husband has a long-standing interest in the genetics of the alpaca breeds and in the science of building their own herd, in part because his father helped facilitate the initial llama movement several years earlier. Michael has literally written the book on alpaca breeding in North America and has published three renowned books on the subject.

In 1990 when the Safleys moved the Northwest Alpacas Ranch to Hillsboro, Oregon, their herd had grown to 100 head. "You breed them every year until your stock multiplies. If you sell too many, you buy more," says Julie. At one point their herd reached 500 head, but today they prefer to keep the stock around 300 animals.

Each year of breeding will typically produce just one offspring per female and the gestation takes almost an entire year. A baby alpaca is called a cria. A newborn female cria won't be ready to reproduce for at least 18 months.

Julie adds that their ranch's growth reflects how the industry as a whole has grown tremendously in the past couple of decades. Thanks to the Safleys' efforts, along with those of the other alpaca pioneers, today there are more than 75,000 registered alpacas nationwide.

From the beginning, Julie was attracted to the multifaceted appeal of the alpaca fiber. Her love for fibers came from her childhood exposure to her great grandfather's sheep ranch, which was the largest Oregon operation of its kind in his day. She carried her fascination with fibers into adulthood and was very active in the high-profile fashion industry and couture markets on both the East and West Coasts before settling into her marketing role on the ranch.

In comparison to the more common natural fibers, such as wool and cotton, that most consumers in North America are used to, alpaca fiber is much stronger, warmer, and softer. It has a feel and durability similar to cashmere, which is considered a luxury fiber. Alpaca hairs have air pockets along each shaft that trap body heat. Therefore, alpaca hair is different than the solid composition of the cashmere goat hairs, which needs more than one fiber to lock in body heat.

Due to the unique nature of the alpaca's coats, new owners didn't exactly know where to begin with harvesting the fiber in the early days of the U.S. industry. "When the alpacas were first brought into the U.S., breeders didn't want to shear them because the alpaca was so gorgeous in full fleece and it made them look so spectacular. These animals went for five or six years without breeders shearing them. It's not good

Initially, alpaca owners didn't want to shear alpacas and use the fiber; however, today alpacas are shorn once each year. This alpaca has been recently shorn.

Julie created the Alpaca Fiber Cooperative of North America to help alpaca farmers gain the most value out of their fiber harvest.

for the health of the animal. It's terrible for the fiber; you wind up not being able to do anything with it. Alpacas need to be shorn once a year just like sheep," Julie explains.

According to Julie, many owners were worried about the aesthetic values of the shorn alpacas, thinking they wouldn't sell for as high a price without their coats. "I think the animals are beautiful either way," she insists.

Looking back to Julie and Michael's early experiences raising the alpacas, she laughs a bit and says emphatically, "It's definite teamwork." Even her husband was a bit apprehensive about harvesting the fiber at first. "When even he didn't want to shear them at first, I finally said, 'Please, let's give this a try.' So we sheared the entire herd and have continued since."

To help further the cause of convincing other owners it was time to start the regular shearing, Julie and Michael placed pictures of their own stock in an issue of the Alpaca Owners and Breeders Association's *Alpacas Magazine*. "We did a full-page ad in the magazine of our animals shorn head to toe. Little by little, breeders started shearing. But, you know it's a funny thing. They started shearing them like poodles," Julie says about the owners who left some of the second and third cuts of fiber on the animals. "They didn't want to shear their full fleece. Several breeders wouldn't shave their legs or their necks."

Julie says it took years of education among the owners and members within the breeders' association before annual full shearing really caught on. "It was all education,

so I started a newsletter to share sources and educate breeders about the care and processing of alpaca fiber." With the help of a family friend and fellow alpaca expert, Cameron Holt, of the Melbourne Institute of Textiles in Australia, Julie also wrote and published a couple of *Clip Care Manuals* for the association.

Thanks to the alpaca pioneers, including Julie and Michael, there are over 60,000 registered alpaca in the United States.

Julie worked very hard to found a fiber cooperative—the Alpaca Fiber Cooperative of North America—to help the growing number of alpaca owners get the most value from their annual harvests. She remained active in both the association and the cooperative until 2001. At that time, she resigned to focus her time and attention on caring for her ailing parents, the 80-acre ranch, and her four teenage children. Despite her love for the marketing of alpacas, Julie says there came a point when it was time for her to put her family first. "Several farm woman I have known have reached that point," she says.

Each year, Julie and Michael make time for their annual trip to Peru to meet with the people of the villages where the stock of alpacas they raise was originally started. Michael is driven by his desire to do more genetic research, and Julie enjoys the opportunity to satisfy her curiosity in the latest Peruvian-made alpaca products.

Alpaca fiber is used for many purposes. This cat loves to snuggle up on this beautiful alpaca blanket.

When Julie gathers her own alpacas' fiber during shearing, she first sorts it by the grade and color of the fibers. "Alpacas come in 22 natural colors, and you can condense those down to about seven: white, light fawn, fawn, rose-grey, silver-grey, brown, and black," she says. "For example, you sort all the different brown tones together to achieve one particular brown for the season; it'll be different the next season."

"Each animal produces its own individual color," Julie says. "And then each alpaca has a different micron count, which determines the fineness of their fiber." Julie and Michael breed for specific fiber traits, but they're still sometimes surprised from hidden generational genetics that may come out in the color of the animal.

Today there are more than 1,000 members in the co-op that Julie helped establish, and that is where she currently sends her fiber. The co-op decides what to do with members' harvests, and whether to turn it into products or sell it to other countries. "Individual alpaca owners can also decide to do what they want to with their fiber," says Julie.

One option owners do have is to send the fiber to a yarn mill. Initially, Julie did extensive research to find a mill in New Mexico to spin her alpaca fiber into yarn. She brought the yarn back to Oregon to provide local fiber artists the material to knit sweaters and weave specialty items, such as blankets.

Julie sold a combination of handmade products from the local artistry and commercially made Peruvian merchandise in a 100-year-old dairy barn on their ranch, which she had renovated into the Northwest Alpacas Country Store. It was the first shop to exclusively feature alpaca products in America. Although her local merchandise was more expensive, she felt it filled the cottage industry niche. Conversely, Julie satisfied the demand from the more mainstream customer, "Someone who might just want a simple black alpaca sweater to wear to the office," with her imports.

Because of her commitment to caring for her family and the alpacas, Julie closed her store a few years ago but she plans to reopen its doors in the near future. She says it's one of the best ways for her to marry her inherent fashion design talents and her passion for promoting the alpaca fiber.

"I believe the best marketing tool for selling alpacas is through promoting their fiber. If you have a country store on your ranch, that's a welcoming for people. They can visit and learn about the animals and ask questions. Otherwise they might shy away from entering your driveway. This way they can get a close up view of the alpacas and the adorable new babies. It's the luxurious fiber that really sells the animal."

Julie and Michael started out with five alpacas, and at one point their herd had grown to 500 alpacas. Today they keep around 300 animals on their farm.

Michelle Bienick
Applegate, Oregon

By Lauren Heaton

Michelle Bienick and her husband Brian operate a seven-acre farm in the Applegate River Valley in Oregon.

Opposite Page:
Michelle and Brian grow organic vegetables that are sold to local restaurants and at farmers' markets.

On almost any day of the year on her farm in southern Oregon, Michelle Bienick can expect to have her hands in the soil and the sun on her back, willing her to align with the pulse of the earth. She has never felt better or healthier than she does among the flaming orange of her calendula plants and the verdant green of the kale and lettuce leaves that she grows tall and full in a mineral-rich valley. Michelle chose a lifestyle of natural wellness and she knows, looking at her plump 3-month-old son, Jaia Sol, that she will be a farmer forever.

The number of systems Michelle has in orbit on the seven-acre farm she operates in the Applegate River Valley is enough to make some days fuller than 24 hours will allow. She and her husband, Brian, grow several dozen varieties of vegetables for sale at local restaurants and farmers' markets. They grow over 100 varieties of medicinal herbs, from which Michelle makes and sells herbal remedies. They raise chickens and goats, and they make cheese, salsas, and vegetable sauces to trade for organic meats and tilling services from neighboring farmers. The farm feeds the family for the entire year.

Thinking back to the naïve confidence that convinced Michelle and her husband to buy a raw piece of land and begin tilling it while they lived in a tent and bathed in

Chickens, as well as goats, roam around the Bienicks' farm.

their wheelbarrow, she wonders if they weren't plain crazy. Yet, no matter how unorthodox the path was that they took to get here, Michelle knows she is exactly where she belongs.

"I feel so strong, vital, and healthy, and when I look at my baby and see he's so strong, I know it's because of the way we eat," she said. "Without a doubt, this is the most fulfilling way of life for me. To feel that connection with Mother Earth, it's part of my spiritual path."

Michelle didn't plan to become a farmer. She went to college at Illinois State University in the mid-1990s to become a doctor and help people in their healing processes. But over the course of a pre-med program based on prescription medication, she began to feel that something was missing. She knew that the current state of human health would not be rescued by drugs and that there must be another way. One day her curriculum advisor handed her a brochure about the National College of Naturopathic Medicine in Portland, Oregon. "I started crying," Michelle said. "I knew that was what I wanted to do."

Moving to the West Coast was an awakening for Michelle, who learned not only alternative healing methods, but was also introduced to different styles of massage and body work, natural childbirth, progressive ways of gardening, and the importance of eating organic food. She realized that mainstream culture was leading people away

Michelle and Brian's first home on the farm was a tent. They built this yurt after they had constructed a greenhouse and established their farm. They currently live in a straw-bale house that Brian built.

from nature and that the remedy was to rekindle the crucial relationship between human health and real food.

Michelle graduated from the school of natural medicine in 2001, which was supplemented with studies in midwifery and organic gardening along the way. While she was in school, Brian had worked on a medicinal herb farm near Portland and they both longed to get started with their own piece of land. They headed for the sunny south of

Michelle's natural lifestyle radiates in the health of her 3-month-old son, Jaia Sol.

Oregon and purchased a partly wooded parcel with contour and a stream running through it.

Before they even had a home, the Bienicks got to work in the dirt. In their minds, the farm came first. They began by building a 100-foot greenhouse and preparing the ground for a large crop of tomatoes and basil. They camped on the land, cooked over

campfires every night, and lived a simple, sweet life; just the two of them. They learned mostly by doing and their life as farmers matured from there.

The Bienicks supply two area organic restaurants year-round with lettuce, kale, broccoli, basil, carrots, and tomatoes. Food for Thought, an organic eatery in Jacksonville, and the Applegate River Ranch House in Applegate, both strive to support local agriculture and buy produce from the Bienicks as needed.

The 30 chickens raised in a large pen on the farm produce an average of 18 to 20 eggs per day, which the family eats and sells, along with the excess of other vegetables at a local farmstead known as the Whistling Duck. Michelle milks her two LaMancha goats every day and uses the milk for drinking and to make cheese and yogurt.

In addition to vegetables, the farm is heavily peppered with medicinal herbs that Michelle uses for patients she sees at the farm and at the two naturopathic clinics where she used to practice in the valley. Among her most plentiful are the calendula plants, which are often used for healing skin wounds and soothing rashes. Dandelion root and red clover top detoxify the liver and purify the blood. Burdock root makes for a good liver cleanser, as well as a tasty treat when shaved and sautéed in olive oil and

The lush vegetables that thrive on Michelle's farm are proof of her love and appreciation of Mother Earth.

NEXT PAGE:
Since Jaia's birth, Michelle stays at home full-time and is a constant witness to the miracles that happen on the farm.

tamari. Michelle also grows immune-support herbs, such as astragalus and echinacea, and ashwaganda, an Ayurvedic plant with a root that is good for adrenal support and alleviating stress.

Most of the herbs are dried and infused with olive oil to use as a tincture. Many of them are edible, as well as pretty, and the Bienicks add them to their salad mixes. The herbs also serve a dual purpose; many insects and animals that might otherwise harm the garden are offended by their strong odor and taste. Dill and nasturtium keep hungry aphids at bay, and the moles and gophers that make nasty air pockets underground don't like castor beans and elderberry twigs. When the pests get really aggressive, the Bienicks consider it fair play to threaten them with their own urine.

Although nature's opportunists can never be tamped out completely, Michelle plans ahead by simply planting extra. She knows a certain amount of her crop each season will be eaten by the underground bandits.

Whatever money the Bienicks make from selling crops is put right back into the operation to buy seed and irrigation supplies, repair the greenhouse, and pay for the gas to haul their crops to market. Michelle wants to be able to grow the food she feeds her family with her own hands, and selling part of the crop enables her to support her agricultural way of life. But the family does not sustain itself entirely off the land.

Brian works with a straw-bale construction crew during the day, and until Jaia was born, Michelle worked full-time at the clinic. The family also has several tenants whom they consider family. Naba Goldfedder lives on the farm in a yome, which is a combination yurt and canvas dome. Naba works in the area as a glass artist. Several months ago, Rachel and Greg Hanzel moved into the yurt that the Bienicks lived in on their property before Brian built them a straw-bale home. The Hanzels also work during the day; Greg is a teacher and Rachel is a fruit farmer.

Michelle is the only one who farms full-time now, with Jaia on her hip. She left her formal practice after the baby was born and now can only do half of the work she did before. Having extra help has made all the difference, she said. Michelle manages the operation and does as much as she can until the others come home to work in the evenings.

The Applegate Valley's farming community has been invaluable in terms of offering advice, support, and camaraderie for the Bienicks, whose property is isolated by the hills that surround the farm. The family frequents potluck dinners with the younger farming families in the area, and they talk about their common problems and share tricks of the farming trade.

The older-generation farmers, such as the Bienicks' neighbors Mori and Mary, retired cattle ranchers now in their 80s, also have wisdom to pass along to younger farmers who aren't likely to know the history of the area. They recall weather patterns and tell stories of forest fires, bobcats, cougars, and bears that have sometimes caused problems for people and their crops.

Each of the farms has niche goods to trade with the neighbors and Michelle uses her squash soup and garlic sauce to trade for honey and lamb meat. "It's so beautiful to be able to trade with your neighbors and not use money," she said.

Michelle's life is ideal in many ways, but being responsible for maintaining a running farm also has its drawbacks. Someone has to be home every day to feed the chickens and the goats, and the greenhouse needs to be watered twice a day. It's a constant demand, Michelle said, and it means the family can't just pick up whenever they feel like it and go camping or take a weekend trip.

Neither Michelle nor Brian had much formal training on how to run a farm, and they have mostly had to learn by trial and error how to handle unexpected problems with pests and water shortages. They read old farmer's almanacs, talk to other farmers, and have learned to trust their intuition. They have learned a lot by tuning into the

plants, watching how they respond to water and light exposure, and making adjustments based on the language of nature. "We listen and they tell us how they want to grow," Michelle says.

Since she has been home full-time with Jaia, Michelle has watched the worms wiggle through the dirt and marveled at how the plants dance with the sun. While she hasn't been able to do as much of the work, through her stillness she has maintained a more watchful presence on the farm and absorbed her fields' subtle signs of the health. "The farm is happier now, and it shows," she said.

If the family wanted to devote itself entirely to farming and live solely off the land, they would have to produce more and commit to selling at farmers' markets at least three times a week. But Michelle is happy to be able to live the way she has chosen: organic, active, and in step with nature's cycles. "Basically, we're selling food so we can maintain our hobby, but actually it's more like maintaining a way of life."

Michelle trades the produce and products created on her farm with other neighbors in the area for meat and other goods.

Emma Jean Cervantes

La Mesa, New Mexico

By Holly L. Bollinger

When Emma Jean's father became sick, she left her job as a nurse to take over the family farm.

NEXT PAGE:
Emma Jean Cervantes is a third-generation farmer who started out with a small farm that has evolved into the largest and most successful chile-pepper processing plant in the United States. She is pictured here at the New Mexico State University grounds where Emma Jean is actively involved with the horticulture program.

They call her the Queen of the Chile Peppers. She doesn't wear a royal crown or sit upon a gilded throne, but if there was ever an appropriately regal nickname in modern day agriculture, it's the one Emma Jean Cervantes has earned during the past few decades.

She is the president and owner of J. F. Apodaca Farms Co. Inc. and Cervantes Enterprises, Inc., in La Mesa, New Mexico, just south of Las Cruces and west of El Paso, Texas. More accurately and simply put, Emma Jean is a farmer with an entrepreneurial spirit.

"I'm a third-generation agriculturist," Emma Jean says as she describes herself. "Actually, I came from a mother and father that really didn't think that women belonged in the agricultural industry."

Emma Jean most certainly does belong in the industry. In fewer than 30 years, she has established the largest and most successful chile-pepper processing plant in the United States. And that's in addition to farming 1,500 acres of crops, including many varieties of chile peppers, cotton, vegetables, and pecan tree groves.

Her grandparents originally farmed the dry New Mexico land on a very small scale in Old Mesilla. The community of Old Mesilla has since been absorbed by the growing population of Las Cruces, which houses the New Mexico State University. Emma Jean estimates that her grandparents may have worked about 15 or 20 acres of

The NMSU program Emma is involved with grows a wide variety of chiles.

land. When they died, their acreage was split up among their large family. Emma Jean's father sold his share and bought 10 acres of seemingly barren land further south in La Mesa.

In 1930, Emma Jean's parents married and started the J. F. Apodaca family farm. "My father had his beginning from a small farmer that would carry his produce into the city and sell it." She remembers him carting cantaloupes, watermelons, and other produce to town or to a local farmers' market for sale. As his business grew, so did their farm. Emma Jean's father continued to buy land whenever he could afford it. But he wasn't acquiring lush, fertile soils. He worked hard to develop mesquite land. "My father really had meager beginnings," says Emma Jean. "He came to the town La Mesa and actually developed about a thousand acres of what we call undeveloped land into production."

Eventually, her father built up his operation to the point where he also could build a house for his family. Emma Jean still lives in the 5,000-square-foot home that she describes as very much like an authentic hacienda in style and comfort. It is the same today as when she was growing up, and it is where she raised her own family.

"Actually, I've been in agriculture all my life because I lived on the family farm. I followed my father around and learned it since I was a youngster," says Emma Jean. At a young age, her traditional father asked his two daughters to make a major decision about which form of education they would choose to take them off of the farm—one must choose to be a teacher and one to be a nurse. The sisters agreed.

Emma Jean earned her Bachelor of Science degree in Nursing Education from Mount Saint Mary's University in Los Angeles. Immediately, her degree allowed her to reach out to the community back home in a variety of health care educator roles. She went on to teach nursing at New Mexico State University in Las Cruces while she raised her three children on the farm. She spent about 10 years serving the community as a professional nurse.

"I left New Mexico to attend a university in California and then came back and married a fellow from El Paso, Texas, which is pretty close to here. I was always able to keep focus and in touch with farming, although I was not directly involved until my father became ill. But I really felt that I learned it, as well as I could have, from a business point of view."

In the course of his lifetime, Emma Jean's father had grown the family farm to 1,000 acres. When his health failed, Emma Jean became the natural choice to take over the farming business. By that time, Emma Jean says her father had seen her succeed as a nursing leader in the community and was glad to have her interest in handling the family business.

"Today, we grow a lot of varieties of crops, mostly cotton, because our climate and weather really address that crop. We grow alfalfa, which is the hay for the dairies; we have a big valley of dairies here. And we have a lot of pecan trees. Pecans have really become a huge crop, and a lucrative crop, in this valley." And, of course, there are the chiles.

Emma Jean is proud to still be farming the land her father developed. Since taking the farm's reins, she's added another 500 acres to the farming operation. But it was the

Flowers flourish on the NMSU's experimental farm.

addition of the chile processing plant that has set Emma Jean apart in her field, adding value to the agriculture business. "It was about 1990 that we diversified," she says.

Emma Jean admits expanding her business beyond the farm wasn't easy. "I must say it was a real challenge for me because the industry was, to begin with, discriminatory toward women," she says.

Cervantes Enterprises Inc. started doing business with the group in processing the types of chiles that make up Louisiana-style hot sauces, but soon realized it was too labor intensive and expensive to harvest the peppers strictly in New Mexico. That's when her operation started importing fresh chiles for processing from Mexico, under the watchful eye of the U.S. Department of Agriculture's strict trade and quality guidelines.

Emma Jean points out that more than 1,000 brands of hot sauce are sold in the country. "A number of the hot sauce bottles that you see on the shelves, the basis for, actually, may come from New Mexico and possibly even our facility," she says.

One of the less tangible upsides of Emma Jean's success with her chile processing is her visibility and the recognition she's received for her work. "It's projected me more into the industry," she says. "The chile industry has become enormous. The population throughout the world has certainly become aware of the popularity of chile and now it's become very marketable so that it's given me a lot of opportunities for involvement." She's participated on many local, state, and federal trade boards and received

In 1990, Emma Jean decided it was time to diversify and start processing the chile peppers. The chile peppers are pulverized in a hammer mill.

numerous awards for her work to promote the different varieties and to preserve the future of chile crops and value-added products through research and development for the growing and processing industries.

What the hot sauce providers actually get from Cervantes Enterprises Inc. is more of a chile paste/mash, which provides them with a basis for their finished product that they in turn add specific ingredients to the bottle.

Although the most popular variety of chile for sauces is the cayenne variety, Emma Jean explains there is still an art to the delicate blends of raw chiles that make each specific brand name's end results taste so unique. "We address everybody's recipes.

The mash created from the pulverized chile peppers is stored in these 21,000-gallon tanks. Cervantes Enterprises uses 300 storage tanks.

Every company has its own specifications." Some companies continue bottling with their original recipe, but also for variety, they create blends of other chiles like the habanero, which is the most intensely spicy chile and recognized among the hottest peppers in Scoville units (usually rating between 100,000 and 350,000 Scoville units), and the chipotle, which is basically a jalapeno that is usually smoked dry in the red stage to achieve a distinct flavor.

The process of making the mash is laborious and time-intensive. Emma Jean says her plant processes chiles almost 20 hours a day for up to four months. The hand-picked, destemmed fresh chile peppers arrive on huge trucks from Mexico, as well as

Emma Jean is honored in the Chile Pepper Institute's Hall of Flame.

from her acreage on the farm. The nearly 50,000 pounds of chile pods from each truck are washed, undesirable and imperfect chiles are removed, and finally, the selected peppers pass through an intense hammer mill where they're pulverized and piped into 21,000-gallon fiberglass tanks. Emma Jean says, "Currently we have 300 storage tanks which we ship out of year round in milk-style tanker trucks or 55-gallon barrels to the customer."

When the mashing processes are in full swing, Emma Jean says any passersby would know it. The aroma released by the process can cause even the most seasoned spice-loving aficionados to tear up and cough their way through the plant.

Emma Jean says they begin working the fields for the year's planting season around the first of January. Most of our product is contracted a year in advance in order to develop a crop plan and meet consumer demand. "Before we put the seed in the ground, we have to know our budget and needs for the year," she says.

"We grow chile from seed, and some of the varieties that we grow are very expensive," she says. Some of the more expensive varieties are grown into seedling stage in the farm's greenhouse and then transplanted in the ground in April after the danger of low temperatures has completely subsided.

Throughout the intense growing season that lasts from April through July, irrigating the chile is essential. Emma Jean's crew constantly monitors the plants and relies on the expertise of a staff entomologist to make sure the chile crop is growing according to schedule. If the seasonal rains come too early in April and May, the plants are more susceptible to a devastating disease, brought on by hungry leafhoppers, that could potentially destroy the crop.

The end of the growing season is a particularly tense time for Emma Jean because she says that a yield is always the key to her farm's continued success. Harvesting chile peppers at just the right time is essential.

Processing usually takes place by the first of August. Once it has started, processing continues seven days a week to capture the full window of opportunity following the harvest. Peppers have a low tolerance for freezing and the chile season is over when the first frost hits.

The chile processing plant is surrounded by about 500 acres of Emma Jean's now-1,500-acre farm enterprise. She estimates 600 of the 1,000 acres that she started with are together on a big parcel of land. The other acreage is in clusters, each within a handful of miles from her office or home.

Maintaining good relationships and her business reputation among her suppliers means more opportunities to increase the volume of chiles she processes each year. "Obviously, I want the business to grow. I hope we can accomplish to process more and more of the chile. And that means expansion and growth," she says decidedly. "I expect to grow in the business."

Another place that Emma Jean wants to see growth is in the entire chile industry. She says most of the industry itself is very family-oriented and that she's learned so much from meeting the other families owning businesses that were handed down and who continue to succeed.

It's no secret that having her grown children close to home makes Emma Jean's life's work even more enjoyable. Her oldest, Joseph, is a Las Cruces attorney and state representative who helps out on the occasional legal paperwork that needs to be handled. The middle child, Dino, is now the general manager, and her daughter, Kristina, is a leader in the marketing arm of the family business. "It certainly lessens my stress as far as lines of succession," she says. "They're learning the business intensely so they can just take it right over once I do not participate."

Emma Jean is hesitant to say when that time will come. "I love what I do. I'm very driven. I think that I got a lot of my mother and father's mentoring because they were very hardworking and they loved what they did."

"I think one of my dreams would be that I would mentor some of my grandchildren who would continue the business," Emma Jean muses in reference to her six granddaughters. "It's only a dream." If there's anything that Emma Jean has learned throughout her life, it's that dreams do come true.

"My whole history has been, you can almost say, a life-changing experience," Emma Jean says about herself. "When I look back, I think, 'Wow, this farm operation has survived since 1930?'"

As she sees other businesses and farms come and go, Emma Jean continues to be grateful that her family is keeping the farm going together. "What is so unique, and I'm very fortunate, is that I still have all of my family here. I'm very fortunate because my children are continuing the legacy. And that's probably what I'm most proud of is my legacy in agriculture and family values."

From April to July, Emma Jean's workers keep a constant eye on the plants during the growing season.

Maud Powell

Jacksonville, Oregon

By Lauren Heaton

In the hills of southern Oregon's sun-drenched Rogue River Valley, it is not so much the exception as the rule to see small organic farms cropping up between hamlets to supply the local farmers' markets, restaurants, and grocery stores with fresh, hand-picked tomatoes, dill, and peaches. Yet, if organic growers ever hope to gain footing as a competitor of the conventional farming industry, they will have to organize and work toward a unified vision, such as the one Maud Powell has set in motion for her farm community in Jacksonville. She is the organic grower's scout; the one who plans how to tackle the next ridge and sustain the next farming generation.

For seven years, Maud and her husband, Tom, have farmed five acres on the slope of a rocky forest they own with Maud's sister and brother-in-law, Lucinda and Dicken Weatherby. The Powells coordinate a community-supported agriculture cooperative (CSA) involving nine local farms, seven of which supply organic vegetables, eggs, milk, cheese, meat, and flowers to over 75 families in the valley. The Powells are also beginning to explore the market for growing organic heirloom vegetable seeds to sell to organic seed distribution companies.

The CSA supplies organic food for a lot of people in the community, but Maud tends to think beyond her immediate area. She looks at the population of the entire Rogue Valley and wonders what steps the organic growers should take in order to one day be able to feed the 120,000 people that live there. The Willamette Valley near Eugene does well with larger-scale organic farms of 50 acres each, she said. And if they can do it, Maud believes it's just a matter of time before her area catches up to it.

The Powells' farm is one of nine farms in the CSA that provide produce for 75 subscribers. There is a waiting list for people who want to subscribe to the CSA.

Maud traveled halfway across the world to discover her passion for farming. While trekking through India in 1997, she and her husband learned of an opportunity to integrate as temporary laborers in an agricultural area high on the plateau of Ladakh in northern Kashmir. They became part of a relief program to mitigate the effects of global trade and help sustain traditional farming families whose children were being drawn to work in urban areas of India.

Neither Maud nor her husband had ever farmed before, but they took up the yak plow anyway. For three months, they helped nurse fields of barley, wheat, potatoes, and hearty vegetables through the harvest. It was a completely nonmechanized operation dependent on animal and manual labor. They lived with a family that included four generations all under one roof, and they fell in love with the communal way of farming.

When it was over, they both knew they wanted to join the league of farmers in their home country. "Being there was hugely inspiring, and it was a huge turning point," Maud said. "We knew we had found our passion in life."

In Ladakh, they witnessed how the centralization of the world's food supply had profound negative affects for people who had been self-sufficient for hundreds of generations. The threat to independent American farmers who struggle to compete with the cheap, industrial food production business was not so different. Maud and her husband felt compelled to do something about it.

They headed to Oregon, where Maud's family had relocated from the East Coast, and interned at two organic farms that were part of a CSA. They learned about succession planting to maintain the soil's nutrients, drip tape irrigation to conserve water in the high desert summers, and saw how farmers were cooperating in order to sustain through their CSA.

After nine months of training, the Powells and the Weatherbys purchased 180 acres of land, built a straw-bale house with wings for both families, and began to plow their fields with a brand new subsoiler.

Contrary to what they had expected because of the community farming tradition in Ladakh, their initial foray into farming was very lonely. Why weren't they sharing meals with their neighbors and talking about their crops, they wondered, and where were the yaks to plow and the donkeys to carry? Maud especially missed the relationships Ladakhis have with their animals. "We had some chickens, but it's hard to have a relationship with chickens," she said.

Another major challenge for Maud was developing an equal partnership with Tom on the farm while they were trying to raise a family. The Powells had their daughter Grace, now 7, just after they moved to the farm. Their son, Sam, came four years later in 1999.

"The first few years were challenging because suddenly we were really having a baby and trying to farm at the same time. It was pretty frustrating," Maud says. "And suddenly the farming turned into this very gendered situation."

While Maud nursed, Tom went ahead with the farm and conquered a steep learning curve without her. Maud fell behind and soon Tom could do things much faster, so it simply made sense for him to do them. "It was very disheartening," Maud explains.

NEXT PAGE:
The five acres of rocky slope that the Powells' live on and farm are co-owned by Maud's sister and brother-in-law, Lucinda and Dicken Weatherby.

Maud and Tom use heirloom seeds on their farm and are working to expand the organic and heirloom seed market in southern Oregon.

Maud kept on with her commitment to the farm, however. Eventually she found both the support of the farming community she'd been looking for, as well as her strength in leadership and organization that has been important for many organic farmers in the area.

The Powells' CSA is a cooperative venture between nine organic farms in the Rogue River Valley who each provide a slightly different variety of produce, meat, and dairy products to its subscribers. The Powell farm covers the root vegetable niche, including carrots, beets, onions, potatoes, winter squash, parsnips, and rutabagas.

A young couple who helps out on the farm lives in this yurt.

Tom is responsible for coordinating the growers to ensure that a mix of different foods gets to their subscribers. Every Wednesday, he packs 75 boxes and delivers them to six pick-up locations in the valley, including one stop at a local nonprofit organization that supplies fresh organic food for about 100 low-income seniors. On average, each box feeds one family for a week. Each week, the CSA provides 75 boxes for individual families, plus 10 to 15 boxes for its seniors.

Grace now helps the family by packing boxes in the greenhouse and accompanying Tom on his deliveries. "Our son is more of a saboteur at the moment," Maud said.

Complementing Tom's quiet, steady work style, Maud has found she is good at looking at the big picture. She finds opportunities to grow the CSA and make it a more profitable, sustainable organism. Maud returned to school after Grace was born to get a graduate degree in the Environment and Community program at Antioch University in Seattle. After that, Maud had the credentials to secure a rural development grant from the U.S. Department of Agriculture for a feasibility study on growing organic heirloom seeds in her area.

As the large-scale mechanized farming industry has grown, the variety in heirloom seeds has been lost to a production system that relies on predictability and consistency. To yield the biggest profit, large agribusinesses grow only the varieties of crops that can be picked with a machine, withstand weeks of transport, ripen at the same time, and arrive at the grocery store at least looking the part. Taste is a secondary issue, if not entirely beside the point.

Seeds of Change, a well-known organic seed and food company that supports the diversification of seed varieties, approached the Powells in 2001 about growing 200 pounds of heirloom variety onion seeds. Southern Oregon's dry summers are perfect for preventing seeds from molding, and small farms can easily produce that amount of seed on just a half an acre. Their yield was good, and this year the Powells will grow seeds for two lettuce crops, sunflowers, onions, beets, and red and daikon radishes. They will sell them to Seeds of Change and to Fedco, a cooperative seed and garden supply company that distributes both organic and conventional seeds.

The feasibility study helped others in the co-op begin growing seeds as well, and Maud is now working to grow the organic seed market in the southern Oregon area.

Maud hopes that in time the Rogue Valley CSA will provide enough food for all 120,000 people in the area and strengthen the local economy.

She has written state and other grants to allow the co-op to purchase a $10,000 seed cleaning apparatus, provide technical support to improve the seed quality, and help growers market their seeds.

Maud's focus on the future of the CSA has been good for the group and for her, she said. "The co-op needed someone to take a leadership role and I like

Three ponds were built on the property to collect rainwater that is used to irrigate the crops via a drip tape system.

thinking more long-term, on a broader scope, about what the community needs to move forward."

The good news for organic growers is that the demand for whole foods in southern Oregon continues to grow. The people of the Rogue River Valley want fresh, organic produce, said Maud, whose co-op has a waiting list of people who want to subscribe. The issue is about the supply. There are not enough organic farmers settling in the area to feed everyone, and very few of the existing farms are over 10 acres.

To be sure, in Maud's view, a moderately sized organic farm can be productive, profitable, and still support biodiversity to remain a part of the local economy. But many of the organic farms that produce on a massive scale and ship their produce all around the country are interested in those same predictable seed varieties. They don't necessarily farm in an ecologically responsible manner and pay little or no attention to conserving resources or protecting the waterways and wildlife corridors around them. Very little of their profit is invested back into their local economies. According to Maud, 90 cents of every dollar spent on organic lettuce at Wal-Mart leaves the community where it was purchased. "It's important to distinguish between organic food grown in an industrial way in California, for instance, versus the small-scale organic farmers around here," she said. "The biggest issue is what do you want to support?"

Buying from smaller-scale local growers means almost 100 percent of the purchase price is going into the pockets of neighbors and supporting the local economy. Powell believes this is a good thing. She hopes that keeping regional economies strong will prevent the centralization of wealth that forced the Ladakhi people to buy cheap government food subsidies because they could not sell enough of their own traditionally produced crops to purchase their other material needs. The erosion of the local

Maud is very passionate about her belief of feeding the world's population by small-scale subsistence farming.

food economy there has challenged what used to be a self-sufficient community with a rich cultural heritage.

Practicing agriculture on a moderate scale helps preserve the environment. For example, Maud's farm is certified salmon-safe, meaning it is a 100 percent organic farm that has taken the extra step to protect the riparian corridors on the banks of the rivers and streams where salmon and other species spawn. This level of commitment to the environment means farmers must keep their animals away from sensitive areas and maintain the trees that keep the water cool and prevent erosion.

The Powells utilize other ecological farming practices to conserve resources. They built three ponds on their property to collect rainwater, which they use to irrigate their crops through drip tape, a system that uses much less water than the traditional overhead irrigation systems. Since they farm on the contour of a slope, they cannot use a cultivating tractor and must do all their weeding by hoe and hand. Their subsoiler is a water-conserving tiller.

To supplement the farm, Tom runs a small irrigation business at which he designs and installs irrigation systems for area farmers. Maud works 15 hours per week for the co-op. Between the two of them, they manage to pay for the farm and save just a little. They have found that farmers' markets are not financially feasible because they require large chunks of time, which neither one has, to sell retail.

Although the Weatherbys and their children, Jasper and Kevin, don't farm, their contributions toward the mortgage and investments in capital improvements for the property have helped make the whole thing possible. It has taken Maud's father a while to understand the appeal of the farming life. Tom's father, who grew up on a subsistence farm during the Depression, was astonished when the couple decided they would live off the land. But the families have become interested in the Powells' choice of crops and they have shown more enthusiasm each year the farm grows.

Maud and her husband still believe that small-scale agriculture is the only sustainable way of feeding the world's population. They are committed to doing their part to educate and be an innovative model for future growers. In the end, Maud farms because she is passionate about the land, and she has found she has a role to play in making organic foods more widely available for others.

Maria Largaespada

Jacksonville, Oregon

By Amy Glaser

The vineyard consists of 5,000 plants on 10 acres outside of Jacksonville, Oregon.

OPPOSITE PAGE:
For eight months out of the year, Maria Largaespada spends every day tending the plants in her vineyard.

As the sun rises over the southern Oregon vineyard, Maria Largaespada looks out over her acres of grapevines and begins her day. For eight months of the year, Maria constantly tends her 5,000 plants on 10 acres, but every day she lives out a dream.

Very few people enjoy the luxury of having their dream job be their everyday reality. Maria is one of the lucky ones. With their children nearing high school graduation and preparing to leave for college, Maria asked her husband, Matthew Sorenson, "If you could do anything you wanted, what would it be?"

His reply, "Grow grapes and make fine wine."

That simple dream is now Maria's lifestyle. At the time of Matthew's revelation, Maria had spent 20 years in the pharmaceutical industry in Indianapolis, and Matthew was a chemist. Neither had a clue about what running a vineyard entailed, so they hit the books. During the planning process, they had decided that Maria would tend to the vineyard while Matthew would stay in Indianapolis and work to maintain a steady income. After three years of researching and planning, they bought a vineyard near Jacksonville, Oregon, in 1999. Maria and Matthew had never been to southern Oregon, and they fell in love with the area during their first visit. The region's conditions suit wine making. The Mediterranean-esque climate is relatively temperate and

Maria tends to every plant by hand. The only tasks on the farm that are not done by hand is mowing between the rows and spraying the plants with sulfur to prevent mildew.

the area receives the right amount of rain (25 inches a year) for a vineyard to thrive. The lightly populated area's vineyards and annual events such as the Shakespeare festival attract a steady stream of tourists.

Maria and Matthew named their vineyard LongSword—the English translation of Maria's surname. Originally planted in 1982, the land had evolved into an established vineyard by the time of their purchase. It had sat unattended for a few years before the

When the grapes are ripe, Maria hires a crew of 15 people to help with the picking.

sale, so Maria and Matthew's first task was attending to desperately needed maintenance, which required a lot of time and patience. The couple updated the irrigation system, put in a new trellis, and implemented a lot of infrastructure in order to get the LongSword Vineyard up and running.

Maria and Matthew met some wonderful friends through their real estate agent, one of whom was Sarah Powell, an accomplished winemaker. She became an influential mentor to Maria. Working with Sarah convinced Maria to begin producing wine under the LongSword label. Originally, they only sold their grapes to other wineries. They started making their own wine in 2002. The wine business has thrived, and last year they opened a patio that invites people to stop by, have a glass of wine, sit, and relax in the shadow of the vineyard.

Owning a vineyard may sound romantic and idyllic, but for eight months of the year, Maria works hard attending to her plants. During the other four months of the year when the grapes are dormant, Maria heads back to Indianapolis to spend time with her husband, who still has his day job as a chemist. In the late winter and early spring, she prunes the plants. This tough and tedious task involves trimming 10 to 15 pounds of material off every plant. All is pruned from the plant, except for two canes. Pruning is a precise art form since the remaining cane has to be flexible and the right size. Shoots will grow, and spurs are left for future growth. Maria takes a few weeks to prune all the plants. Every task at the vineyard is done by hand, except for mowing between the rows and spraying, which are done with a small tractor.

In mid-April, the buds break. At this time, frost is a concern. Overhead sprinklers keep the plants wet and at a constant 32 degrees Fahrenheit so the plants don't freeze. On cold nights, Maria gets up during the middle of the night to check the temperature and, if need be, turn on the sprinklers. It's not the most fun to slog around in the cold turning on the sprinklers in the middle of the night, but it's all part of the process of caring for the plants, which Maria loves. The grapes aren't just fruit growing on the vine. "They're my babies," says Maria. She loves watching her plants grow and tending each by hand. She takes pride in her plants and says it's a powerful personal statement and that she is fortunate to have a successful vineyard.

During the summer, the wine patio is open in the afternoons for visitors to stop by and have a glass of wine in the shadow of the vineyard that produced it.

When the buds are 3 to 4 inches long, Maria sprays them with sulfur, which is organically permissible and protects the plants from powdery mildew. The sulfur is sprayed every 10 to 14 days until mid-August to help protect the plants. Maria's vineyard is in the three-year process of its organic certification. She utilizes a no-till system to keep beneficial insects around the plants and prevent erosion. She does mow between the rows with a tractor and cuts the grass underneath the plants with a weed trimmer to keep the weeds down.

The shoots are thinned in late May to early June. For each bud, there is one shoot. When the shoots grow to be 8 to 10 inches long, they are pulled back with a catch line to position the canopy and expose the buds to more sunlight and increase air flow. Water-sucker shoots are cut off at this stage to ensure that the plant puts its photosynthetic energy straight to the grapes and not the leaves. A higher sugar content sweetens and concentrates the flavor of the grapes. Maria takes about two weeks to complete the process for her vineyard.

When the grapes grow larger, Maria secures them with a second catch line to hold the canopy upright and improve air flow once again. When the vines grow too long, hedging is done by hand to cut back some of the vines.

Established vineyards such as Maria's don't need a lot of water. New vineyards do require a lot of water, but dry conditions are actually beneficial at established vineyards because more sugar goes into the grapes instead of into the plant and leaves. "Farming is very dependent on the weather," Maria explains. "You deal with what Mother Nature gives us, and she usually gives us what we need."

The grapes usually ripen anytime from early September to late October. Before this time, Maria constantly checks the grapes to see how they are progressing. To see if the grape is ripe, she crushes the grape and tastes it. However, the most accurate sign that the grapes are ready is the flock of birds that arrive at the vineyard and eat the grapes: "You wouldn't think that birds would eat a lot, but they ate two tons last year." The birds cue Maria to gather a crew of 15 people to go out and pick the grapes by hand as soon as possible. Harvest season is one of the few times Maria hires help on her farm; the rest of the work is done by only Maria. The average amount of grape yield for LongSword is about 30 tons. A big yield isn't always better in the vineyard business; the smaller the yield, the more concentrated the flavor.

Maria's crew usually takes three days to pick the grapes, but it's not three days of constant field work. The picking is done in the early morning while the weather is still cool. If the grapes are exposed to more than a few hours of blazing sun, they will wilt and split, so they are immediately trucked to other wineries three hours away.

Maria sells about half her grapes to other wineries. The rest she makes into two kinds of wine: Invitation, a Chardonnay, and Accolade, a sparkling Chardonnay. She leases a space at another winery and uses its press to make the wine (an arrangement known as custom crush). A typical day for Maria during this time is harvesting in the morning and then heading to the winery to assist in pressing the grapes. The juice settles overnight, the solids are racked off the juice, and then the fermenting process begins with the addition of wine yeast. It takes 10 to 24 days for the wine to ferment. It has to be stirred every day and checked to see how the process is coming along. The wine is then put into barrels for a couple of months to age before bottling.

Maria bottles all her own wine. The sparkling wine needs to be bottled under pressure. She has a machine that will fill four bottles at a time. The labeling process doesn't happen at this time, because the wine is bottled cold and the labels won't stick with the condensation on the bottles. Maria bottles about 600 to 700 cases per year. Each case contains 12 bottles and weighs 50 pounds. She lifts every single case and says one of the perks of farming is that she doesn't need to go to the gym.

For five hours every day during the summer, the tasting patio is open for people to stop by, have a glass of wine, bask in the afternoon sun, and visit with Maria. The good conversation flows as smoothly as the wine served on the patio.

Accolade is one of the two varieties of wine produced by LongSword Vineyard.

The LongSword Vineyard also includes a 12-acre alfalfa field that is part of a conservation program. The field is a popular landing place for skydivers and paragliders. LongSword has a tradition of offering a glass of wine to any daredevil who lands near the vineyard as a celebration of their flight. After the adrenalin rush of jumping out of a plane or gliding through the air, the skydivers and paragliders can relax on the patio and regale Maria and her guests with their adventures.

Moving to the country and working outside all day with the plants was something completely different for Maria. After spending 20 years in a cubicle, now that she's experienced country life on a farm, she said she could never go back to that routine, "Living in the city, you lose a lot not being in connection to the seasons. I never lived in the country, but here you can look up and see the stars and hear the frogs. I think I live in paradise."

Maria's paradise is a humble one. Her abode is a fifth-wheel trailer parked beside the barn. She has no electricity or running water. Even though she admits she would like to have hot running water some day, she embraces the life she has and the people she has met, "This is a friendly area. There are a lot of great people around, great friends. I can't see living back in the city at this point."

Maria has been able to share her connection to the land and the plants with her daughter and mother. Maria's daughter, Melinda Fryman, helped for the summer while she was in college. She helped repair fences and tend to the plants. Maria said, "It was a very special time with her, to work beside her and spend that time with her." When

The Jacksonville area isn't populated, but there are many vineyards and other attractions that bring a multitude of visitors to the area.

Maria first bought the vineyard her mother, Vera Taylor, an avid gardener, came out for six weeks to help out: "It was such a blessing to spend time with her, doing something that we love." Referring to the time spent working with her mother and daughter, Maria said, "I think it's a female thing. It's the nurturing instinct. It was definitely a blessing to share that time with them."

The extreme career and lifestyle change has dramatically changed Maria's life for the better. "It's a labor of love. It's hard work, but I never knew I'd like farming

Maria had never farmed before the 1999 purchase of the vineyard, but it has been a career move that she hasn't regretted for a minute.

so much, but I really do." Farm life and being in the vineyard has been a spiritual experience for her. "I am working with what God gives me. I am privileged to be part of that creation." Maria said her husband will move out to Oregon permanently when he retires and she thinks that he will enjoy the process and lifestyle. It's not an easy life by any means, but the hard work is all part of the experience and she reaps the rewards every day she steps into her vineyard.

Peggy Case
Pagosa Springs, Colorado

By Holly L. Bollinger

You get the feeling you are visiting a bygone era when you drive through the town of Pagosa Springs in southwestern Colorado's Archuleta County, which borders New Mexico to the north. Main Street is lined with a combination of quaint shops and twenty-first century businesses that almost seamlessly operate side by side. The town's major tourist attractions are its therapeutic Great Pagosa Hot Springs, for which the town was named (an Ute Indian phrase *pah gosa*, meaning "water that has a strong smell," is attributed to the bubbling 145-degree-Fahrenheit water's high mineral content) and the Weminuche Wilderness Area, a hiker's fantasy as the largest road-free trekking area in Colorado.

It's hard to believe that this Old West town and its pristine natural treasures are most often visited electronically by modern-day Internet users around the world who view live pictures and streaming video of its seasons through a multitude of web cams positioned throughout its streets and countryside. As you continue up into the San Juan Mountains that surround the small town of just more than 1,600 residents, it becomes easy to imagine that you're on the same path many Native American tribes, settlers, miners, and cattle drivers used for centuries.

Tucked in the mountain range is where you'll find Peggy Case, a third-generational rancher with a strikingly practical, no-nonsense view on living and working her land in the West. Along with her husband, Bob, Peggy owns and operates the Case Ranch that supports cattle grazing and native-grass haying on 240 acres of well-preserved high-altitude wilderness.

Peggy and her husband, Bob, have 17 acres of hayfields that they harvest to sell and to feed their three horses through the winter.

While a typical day for this couple of more than 50 years would be considered arduous and hectic by many, Peggy thinks her way of life is perfectly relaxing. She handles her daily chores with gratitude and a winsome smile.

When asked how her morning is going, she gives a chipper reply. "Well, let's see. So far today, I've moved the cattle and done the dishes, and I'm getting ready to fix the dinner—besides answering the telephone." Then she hints at what the rest of her day may have in store. "I work in the yard, I work for the church, I work for the library, and I water people's plants in town."

Peggy and Bob have worked their ranch for the same 26-year span that they've lived there. They graze a New Mexico cattle owner's herd on most of their land and they reserve 17 acres for growing hay to sell and to feed their three horses through the winter. "We're too high to feed [graze] in the winter," says Peggy. "You can't raise enough hay in the summertime to feed your cattle through the winter."

The growing limits of the elevation for their rangeland mean the Cases have to practice a form of rotational grazing. Because the cattle have, for the most part, been raised with the Cases, Peggy and Bob have the daily task of moving the herd down to a literal science. "All I have to do is stand out on the hill and call them and they come running." Peggy says the whole process takes about 45 minutes. "You get to where you can go out and call the old biddies, and they just come through the gate. If we've had the same bunch for 26 years, we had all those cows as calves."

Peggy somewhat affectionately calls the herd a duke's mixture. "They're red and they're black and they're brown. And they've got white faces and spots and all of that." Most of the cattle are sold off for beef, with the short yearlings usually being sold in the fall of the same year they're born. But Peggy recalls that one year when beef prices were exceptionally high, the owner shipped the cattle straight from the Case Ranch to market.

Peggy's experience tells her just how much grazing the land can handle. The Cases allow their horses to graze for two hours in the morning and two hours in the evening. "We don't want them to get too fat," says Peggy. "And then we give them a leaf of hay at night so they don't eat up the barn. If you know horses like I do, they eat everything in sight." The horses are kept in an open milking barn with a fenced outdoor enclosure so the animals can exercise freely, but avoid the weather and the flies.

Toner Mountain, named after Peggy's grandfather, serves as the background of the Case's ranch.

"In the wintertime, you'll find them standing out in the corral just soaking up the sun," Peggy says.

Ranching is something that comes naturally to Peggy. She learned most of what she knows about ranching from the time she was a little girl. Her dad was raised on the ranch where she lives today. Her grandparents married and homesteaded the land in 1896. Even in the wild and unforgiving turn-of-the-century terrain, Peggy says her grandmother probably didn't think she was leading a particularly difficult existence. "It was a way of life with them," Peggy says. "She was used to farming."

As Peggy tells the story, her paternal Grandfather Toner came out of Clarinda, Iowa, which was a small town in the southwestern part of the state near the Missouri border. Her grandfather's cattle-driving operation ran into Arizona and New Mexico. Her mother's side did the same, and Peggy's two grandfathers were cousins. "My grandfather Miller came by to visit my grandfather Toner. My mother was riding for my grandfather Miller and that's where she met my dad."

When her parents married, they settled on the family ranch, says Peggy. "My folks did ranching and they had cattle because at that time we had range rights. You could run the cattle on the range in the summertime, which would give you all of your land for hay. That way, you could raise enough hay for your cows and sheep."

Because they were starting from scratch, her parents had no choice but to live in an existing sawmill shack on the property. Peggy and her brother were born and raised for several years in the makeshift house. "There are three rooms. One's a kitchen, one's a dining room, and one's a bedroom. That's it," Peggy says, estimating that each room measures about 22 square feet.

Her father started building the family's main house in the late 1930s. "My dad hued the logs," Peggy remembers. "We helped him hue the logs, my brother and I. We weren't very big, but we got out and helped him." She says the family did most of the logging work in the winter when they had time away from farming. In 1940, after the haying was finished in the fall, the family used the derrick hay stacker to lift the logs and erect the house. It took another two years of finishing work before her family could move in.

PREVIOUS PAGE:

For the past 26 years, Peggy and Bob have farmed the land that Peggy's grandparents homesteaded in 1896.

The produce from the garden is canned or frozen to provide the stockpile of food that Peggy and Bob live on during the winter.

The sawmill shack still survives as a reminder to Peggy of her early childhood; it sits behind the log house and eventual additions that make up her present-day home. The three-room outbuilding came to play an unlikely, but important, role in Peggy's later life.

"My husband and I came back (from college) and we lived in there for three years," says Peggy. She met Bob Case while square dancing one night during her senior year at Colorado A&M in Fort Collins (now Colorado State University). The pair graduated in 1951; he received a forestry degree and she earned a bachelor's degree in home economics education.

They moved onto her parents' ranch in 1952 and stayed until 1955, when Bob started his long career with the U.S. Forest Service. Although her husband was a forest ranger, the couple's cattle background made them a well-suited choice to take care of more rangeland than forests. The couple moved from place to place, on average every two years, during Bob's 30 years of service.

"I've been all over the state and two or three others," Peggy says, taking a deep breath before she begins recounting her travels. "We started out in Utah, and then we went to Arizona. Then from Arizona to Colorado, two places in Colorado, to two places in Wyoming, one place in South Dakota, and back to four places in Colorado."

During that whirlwind time for the Cases, her aging parents decided to sell their range rights for the ranch. Peggy says they could no longer take care of the animals. By the time Peggy and her own family moved back onto the family ranch in 1980, it had been two decades since free grazing was allowed on the vast rangeland slopes. From the beginning, the Case Ranch provided spring and summer grazing and haying of native grasses, such as red clover, white clover, and timothy hay.

Still, the unpredictability of mountain weather plays a big role in the amount of grazing and haying that happens in an active season. In recent years, Peggy has seen rainfall up to an unheard amount of 9 inches in the summer. Other years, they've faced extreme drought. Peggy especially remembers, albeit not fondly, the drought of 2002. "We just sat around and watched everything burn," she says. "Our hay fields, where we generally get pretty close to 1,000 bales, we got 17."

Peggy is grateful for the opportunity to live on the ranch her family created.

Peggy says although they can survive on her husband's retirement pension, the hay income is important to the operation because it allows them to put money back into the ranch.

Still, Peggy prepares for the worst in every season. In the summer months she cans fresh fruit, as well as green beans and other vegetables from her garden. She says that when she can find fresh corn to her liking, she freezes it for later use. Through the fall and winter, the Cases stockpile a supply of everything essential, including gasoline for the generator, in the event an unexpected blizzard blows up. "It has snowed in July, but that's a rarity," Peggy says with a laugh, adding that the first snow can come anywhere from July to December and that snow doesn't typically stop falling until early May.

The fact that temperatures fluctuate wildly throughout the winter—from an average of 10 to 15 degrees below zero (Fahrenheit) up to highs of around 65 or 70 degrees during the day—isn't a concern for Peggy. Neither are the shifting patterns of annual snowfall amounts, which she feels are attributable to something less sinister than environmental pollution or global warming.

"I would say you're going to see this on a cycle," she says. "Because if you could talk back to my grandfather, he could have told you about when they probably wouldn't have a foot of snow all winter, going back to the early 1900s. Then during the 1930s and 1940s, our average snow depth every winter was 3 to 5 feet of snow on the level. And now we're back to, well, we've seen 3 feet in the last 20 years. We've seen it up to 4 feet. And two winters ago, it never got up to a foot." Peggy says she's confident that nature is only following a precipitation timeline of its own, "I think if you would look back in history, it runs on a cycle."

Like the changing seasons that Peggy feels are predictably unpredictable, she says there is nothing about the challenges of ranching that make her want to do anything different, even with her free time. "I like to play cards. But, oh, my gosh, to play bridge three days a week would drive me crazy. I'm just not geared into that. I like being out; I like the animals; I like the outdoors. I don't like neighbors that close."

But Peggy does like having neighbors she knows, even if the closest is about 5 miles away. In fact, she values a sense of community in her life almost as much as the

For 30 years, Peggy and Bob moved all over the western and southwestern United States because Bob was a member of the U.S. Forest Service. They returned to the Case Ranch, where they had lived for the first few years of their marriage, in 1980.

wide-open spaces of ranching. "We loved every community we lived in, got well-acquainted with the people, got real involved with each one of the communities. With my 4-H work, I can hardly go any place in the state of Colorado that I don't run into a 4-H kid that I knew."

When Archuleta County started its annual county fair in the 1950s, Peggy was there as a volunteer. Later, she started judging 4-H student competitions at the South Dakota State Fair. Peggy's daughter was involved in 4-H throughout her adulthood. Her love for involving children with agriculture led Peggy to a lasting volunteer role with the annual county and state fair events in Colorado, where she was the girls' dorm supervisor for 26 years.

Peggy also worked for three years in Archuleta County Extension office out of Pagosa Springs during in the 1980s to help drive up interest in the 4-H program for the local children. "We got quite a few (4-H chapters) going," Peggy proudly says. She adds that many of the children she encouraged to participate have since grown up and have now brought their own children to the 4-H fold.

As times have changed, so has the sense of community for Pagosa Springs. "Because of the terrain that we live in and the beauty, we are really getting invaded with people moving in," says Peggy in a disheartened tone. "I think they figure that 63 percent of the Archuleta community, or the residents of the county, are here less than six months out of the year. It's awfully hard to get a close-knit community with that."

Peggy estimates that although the mostly wealthy second-home homeowners and landowners are officially part of the county's close to 9,000 population, these residents often don't live in the area outside of the summer months. One of Peggy's closest neighbors, her daughter, has turned the impetuosity of the vacationing community into a lucrative, entrepreneurial caretaking business.

Peggy is happy to have her daughter and her daughter's family living close by. She says she's thankful that the year-round residents make the community feel familiar. "The rest of them are old-timers," Peggy says. She knows most of those multi-generational Pagosa Springs families from when she was growing up.

Although Pagosa Springs is 45 minutes away, Peggy and Bob remain a vital part of its community.

Peggy says she's keeping up with the times, but she does so selectively. She works on a computer and makes use of email, but she's not quite sure of her technological savvy. "I have more stuff in cyberspace than anybody else I think," she jokes.

Peggy also enjoys staying up to date on sports. "People ask, 'What do you watch on TV?'" Peggy says her answer is always the same. "Well, I'm a sports fan. And if I have time at night to watch TV, I watch sports. I go to town for the high school sports. I know most of the kids that are playing. I could sit there all evening and watch them."

Supporting the community is one thing, but driving the 45 minutes each way to town for frivolous entertainment is quite another to Peggy and Bob. "We're such movie goers," she says sarcastically. "I think it's been 10 years since we've been to a movie."

As much as Peggy enjoys life on the ranch, so do many others who make the trip from out of town and even out of state to call the Case Ranch home, even if just for a few days. Peggy says their door is always open, and with just a phone call, they're ready to welcome visitors—whether it's a set of friends just passing through on vacation or family coming to join the annual Toner family reunion. She especially looks forward to seeing her extended family during the reunion. More than 50 of Peggy's cousins usually gather at the ranch to commemorate their heritage. In 2006, the family will celebrate the 90th birthday of her oldest living cousin, Lily, who is from what Peggy calls the "first generation" of surviving Toners, the grown children from her grandparents' offspring.

Like many stories of families who settled on what was once envisioned as the Wild West, Peggy life story has been full adventures, hardships, and accomplishments. But at the end of the day, she's more satisfied by the experiences themselves than any one particular outcome. She says she's lucky to be able to enjoy the work of the ranch with her husband, and she sees herself doing just that for the rest of her life. "I think you'll find us right here 'til we die, doing the same thing over and over," Peggy says contentedly. "There hasn't been much we've left undone."

Index